Contact

A series edited by Louis Porcher
Professor at the University « Sorbonne-Nouvelle », Paris

Ber
Véro
Mi

French made easy

A handbook of colloquial French (Intermediate)

45 lessons

HACHETTE F.L.E.
58, rue Jean-Bleuzen
92170 Vanves

"Put a language in your pocket"

Contact

A new series of self-study French courses

General course books and a range of materials designed to meet the specific needs of French learners, providing training in the language along with a mass of interesting information about France and the French.

Already available :

French made easy (beginners)

ISBN : 2.01.018266.9

© Hachette, 1991, 79, boulevard Saint-Germain, F 75006 Paris

THE AUTHORS

Bernard André was born in Versailles in1940 and has taught French to Latin-American students for more than 15 years in Guatemala, Mexico and Peru.
He has written numerous books and articles about the theory and practice of teaching French as a foreign language and is currently working on self-tuition techniques. He also teaches at the university of Paris (Sorbonne-Nouvelle).

Véronique Pugibet, born in Paris in 1955, is a specialist in audio-visual techniques applied to the teaching of French to foreign students. She has worked at the University of Mexico, training future teachers of French.

Michèle Tardy was born in La Rochelle in 1953. A specialist in the teaching of French as a foreign language, she has worked as a teacher in the United States. She is currently teaching at the University of Orléans (France).

Artwork	Chloé PARENT
Layout	ENVERGURE
Editorial assistant	Hélène GONIN
English version	Malcolm SCOTT
Drawings	Emile BRAVO
Cover	
Artwork	Chloé PARENT
Photos	Marcus ROBINSON «Le chien qui fume» : 33, rue du Pont-Neuf, 75001 Paris
Cassettes	
Coordination	Élisa CHAPPEY
Music	Thierry GEOFFROY

CONTENTS

Introduction 6

1 Achats — **Shopping** 10
2 Amour — **Love** 14
3 Animaux — **Animals** 18
4 Argent — **Money** 22
5 Arts — **Arts** 26

Info 1 — *Arriving in France* 30

6 Bar — **Bar** 32
7 Bourse — **Stock Market** 36
8 Centre-ville — **Town Centre** 40
9 Circulation — **Traffic** 44
10 Coiffeur — **Hairdresser** 48

Info 2 — *Travelling in France* 52

11 Corps — **Body** 54
12 Dates — **Dates** 58
13 Douane — **Customs** 62
14 École — **School** 66
15 Famille — **Family** 70

Info 3 — *Mini-guide: the Provinces* 74

16 Fêtes — **Bank Holidays** 76
17 Gastronomie — **Gastronomy** 80
18 Habillement — **Clothes** 84
19 Horaires — **Timetables** 88
20 Hôtel-restaurant — **Hotel-restaurant** 92

Info 4 — *Mini-guide: Paris* 96

21 Invitations — **Invitations** 98
22 Jeux — **Gambling** 102
23 Logement — **Accommodation** 106
24 Médecine — **Medicine** 110
25 Météorologie — **Weather** 114

Info 5	*Cheese and wine*	118
26 **N**ature	**Nature**	120
27 **N**ombres	**Numbers**	124
28 **O**rientation (1)	**Direction (1)**	128
29 **O**rientation (2)	**Direction (2)**	132
30 **P**olice	**Police**	136
Info 6	*Cinema and theatre*	140
31 **P**olitique	**Political institutions**	142
32 **P**oste	**Post office**	146
33 **P**resse	**Press**	150
34 **R**eligion	**Religion**	154
35 **R**enseignements	**Information**	158
Info 7	*Festivals*	162
36 **S**alutations	**Greetings**	164
37 **S**pectacles	**Entertainment**	168
38 **S**ports	**Sports**	172
39 **T**éléphone	**Telephone**	176
40 **T**élévision	**Television**	180
Info 8	*Mini-guide for shoppers*	184
41 **T**ourisme	**Tourism**	186
42 **T**ransports	**Transport**	190
43 **T**ravail	**Work**	194
44 **V**acances	**Holidays**	198
45 **V**oiture	**Car**	202

Grammar summary 206

Verb tables 223

Mini-dictionary (French-English) 237

Mini-dictionary (English-French) 259

Grammar index 281

Index of situations 283

Index of themes 285

French *à la carte*

You have already studied French but you would like to go further and perfect your knowledge of the language : revise a point of grammar, learn how to express yourself on a particular subject... With *French made easy* you design your own course of study in line with your own particular needs and interests.

You will find three indexes at the end of the book : a grammar index, an index of themes and an index of situations (what to say in order to ask for advice, to express a wish...) designed to help you find the lesson(s) containing the information you need at any given moment.

Each lesson stands as an individual unit, written with two objectives in mind : to improve your understanding of colloquial French and your ability to use it.

The book is accompanied by two audio cassettes enabling you to hear authentic French, as it is spoken today.

The book

- 45 lessons based each time on a different theme (money, entertainment, transport, etc.)
- an"info" section : every 5 lessons you will find a double page of useful, practical information to help make a success of your stay in France
- a grammar summary
- verb tables
- a mini-dictionary (French/English - English/French), with more than 1000 entries
- a grammar index
- an index of situations
- an index of themes

The cassettes

- a recording of the texts / dialogues of all 45 lessons
- oral exercises

Because French is also spoken outside a recording studio, we have aimed at the greatest possible authenticity, reproducing the background noises and hesitations of real conversations...

How to use *French made easy*

... to learn to understand

– Use the index to choose the lesson most closely corresponding to your particular needs and interests.
– Listen to the recording of the text, twice at least ... without looking at the book.
– Try to understand the overall meaning, listening carefully for the words you already know.
– Open the book and read the text aloud.
– Check your understanding against the translation and use the mini-dictionary if necessary.

... to enrich your vocabulary

– Learn the 24 words in the vocabulary section by heart ; they complement the words in the text and represent an essential store of words you will need to express yourself on the subject covered in the lesson.

... to revise your grammar

– Study the grammar point(s) contained in each lesson.
– Consult the grammar summary and verb tables for additional information.
– Practise using the structure by completing the 2 written exercises.
– Do the oral exercise recorded on the cassette.
– Check your answers immediately.

... to develop good reflexes

– The section "How to say it!" lists useful expressions for a wide variety of different situations.
– Read the list several times.
– Cover up the original French and try to repeat the expressions from memory using the English translation.

... to enhance your stay in France

– Read the "Bon à savoir" sections devoted to different aspects of French society and culture to learn more about the French way of life.
– Use the "Info" sections as a practical guide for your next visit to France.

Bon courage et à bientôt !

45 lessons

Amour
Corps
Hôtel
Vacances
Argent
Télévision
Sports
Presse
Jeux
Nature
Bar
Spectacles
Politique

– Bonjour, madame. Vous êtes du quartier ? J'ai des courses à faire. Quels magasins vous me conseillez ?
– Il y a beaucoup de commerçants par ici. Pour le pain, je vous recommande la boulangerie au coin de la rue, ils font aussi d'excellents gâteaux pas trop chers. Juste à côté, vous verrez une boucherie-charcuterie et, un peu plus loin, une petite épicerie, ouverte même le dimanche ; ça peut dépanner.
– Et pour des provisions plus importantes ?
– Eh bien, il faut que vous alliez dans un supermarché. Là vous trouverez tout d'un seul coup et ça sera moins cher. Il y a un hypermarché, « une grande surface », dans le centre commercial à la sortie de la ville.

– Good morning, madam. Are you from this part of town ? I have some shopping to do. What shops do you recommend to me ?
– There are lots of tradesmen near here. For bread, I recommend the baker's at the corner of the street ; they also make excellent cakes that aren't too expensive. Just next door, you'll see a butcher's/delicatessen and a little further on, a small grocer's, open even on Sundays. That can be handy.
– And for buying larger quantities of food ?
– Well, you must go to a supermarket. You'll find everything there in one go and it will be less expensive. There's a hypermarket, a « grande surface », in the shopping centre on the road out of town.

BON À SAVOIR

You will find small shops and supermarkets in the centres of French towns while shopping centres ("centres commerciaux") and hypermarkets ("hypermarchés") have sprung up in the suburbs. The most well-known retail distributors are: Carrefour, Leclerc, Auchan, Intermarché, Mammouth ...
It is now possible to do much of your shopping from your living room - via Minitel, a small computer terminal supplied by France Telecom, offering a wide range of services. You simply type in your shopping list, give the number of your credit card to pay for it all, and have the goods delivered by the shop!
The French tend to spend a lot of money on food (a basic pleasure in life!) although other expenses - such as transport and accommodation - are now taking a larger share of the family budget.

VOCABULARY

une boutique shop
un magasin store
un rayon department
une caisse cash desk, till
un ticket (de caisse) receipt
un chariot trolley
un sac bag
une crémerie dairy
une épicerie grocery
une pâtisserie cake shop, pastry
un(e) boulanger(ère) baker
un(e) boucher(ère) butcher
un(e) épicier(ère) grocer
un(e) client(e) customer
un(e) commerçant(e) shopkeeper
un(e) consommateur(trice) consumer
un(e) vendeur(euse) salesman (sales girl)
une caissière cashier
un achat purchase
les soldes sale goods
bon marché cheap
cher expensive
payer to pay
valoir to be worth

GRAMMAR

▮ *The subjunctive of the verb* « aller » :

Il faut que j'aille - que tu ailles - qu'il/elle aille - que nous allions - que vous alliez - qu'ils/elles aillent.

▮ *Use of the subjunctive :*

The subjunctive must be used after :

• **verbs of suggestion, denial, permission :** proposer, refuser, interdire, permettre... *Je propose qu'il s'en aille.* (aller)

– **verbs of wishing and willing :** vouloir, désirer, avoir envie... *Il veut qu'elle fasse ce travail.* (faire)

– **verbs of emotion :** craindre, regretter, avoir peur... *J'ai peur qu'ils ne viennent plus.* (venir)

• **Impersonal verbs and constructions :** falloir, valoir...

• **some subordinating conjunctions :** avant que, bien que, quoique, pour que...

EXERCISES

1. Choose the appropriate word.

courses - soldes - boulangerie - crémerie.

Le pain est bon dans cette ..... . Où vas-tu faire tes ..... ? Cette ..... fabrique son fromage blanc. Tout est trop cher. J'attends les ..... !

2. Make single sentences using the present subjunctive.

Elle doit y aller. Il le faut. → Il faut qu'elle y aille.

Elle doit partir. Il le faut. – Nous devons y retourner. Il le faut. – Tu dois le faire. Il le faut. – Vous devez le savoir. Il le faut.

3. Translate.

Ce boulanger fait du très bon pain. Prenez un chariot à l'entrée du magasin. Il faut que tu ailles faire les courses. Il vaut mieux qu'on le vende.

KEY TO EXERCISES

1. boulangerie - courses - crémerie - soldes.
2. Il faut qu'elle parte. Il faut que nous y retournions. Il faut que tu le fasses. Il faut que vous le sachiez.
3. This baker makes very good bread. Take a trolley at the entrance to the shop. You must go and do the shopping. It's better if we sold it.

HOW TO SAY IT !

DONNER UNE CONSIGNE :

– Passez à la caisse!
– Faites la queue!
– Attendez votre tour, s'il vous plaît!

GIVING INSTRUCTIONS :

– Go to the cashier !
– Stand in line !
– Wait in turn, please !

SE PLAINDRE :

– Il n'y a pas de prix!
– Le prix n'est même pas indiqué!
– C'est trop cher!
– C'est du vol!

COMPLAINING :

– There's no price (on it) !
– The price isn't even marked !
– It's too expensive !
– It's daylight robbery !

Don't hesitate, jump at the offer.
(occasion = opportunity / bargain)

Homme jeune, 40 ans, cadre supérieur, libre, grand, yeux bleus, sportif, élégant, humour, aimant musique, cinéma et voyages, recherche relation solide et durable avec jeune femme 25-35 ans, sensible, jolie et sensuelle pour fonder foyer et faire bébé(s). Adresser réponse (avec photo) au journal qui transmettra.

Youthful man, 40 years old, senior executive, unattached, tall, blue eyes, athletic, elegant, sense of humour, fond of music, the cinema and travelling, looking for a serious, long-lasting relationship with a young woman 25-35, sensitive, attractive and sensual, to build a home and have child(ren).
Send reply (with photo) to the newspaper which will forward.

France often has the reputation among foreigners for being simultaneously the land of romantic love and "libertinage". The French are not always aware of this reputation.

French people nowadays are waiting longer before getting married but are younger when they first live together. Statistically, the number of marriages is increasing, but so is the number of couples getting divorced. Twenty per cent of married couples met at local dances (such as those organised on 14th July) compared with 6.6% who met through friends, 2.8% at night clubs, 2.8% at parties, 1.7% at the beach and 1.2% at the gymnasium ... according to INED statistics ("Institut National des Etudes Démographiques" - National institute of demographic research).

VOCABULARY

un amant	lover
une maîtresse	mistress
un(e) amoureux(euse)	person in love
un(e) copain(ine)	pal, friend
un(e) petit(e) ami(e)	(girl)boy-friend
beaucoup	a lot
passionnément	passionately
une émotion	emotion
une passion	passion
un sentiment	feeling, sentiment
romantique	romantic
aborder	to approach
adorer	to adore
aimer	to love
attirer	to attract
divorcer	to divorce
draguer	to chat up, pick up
embrasser	to kiss
faire l'amour	to make love
flirter	to flirt
plaire	to please
ressentir	to feel
se marier	to get married
se fiancer	to get engaged

Amour

GRAMMAR

■ *Using the «tu» and «vous» form :*

«Tu» is used between friends, by people who know each other very well, between members of the same family.
Tu m'aimes ?

«Vous» is used in formal language, with people older than oneself and with strangers. It is the polite form of address.
Vous êtes libre ce soir ?

■ *Three verbs in the present indicative :*

Pouvoir (to be able) : je peux - tu peux - il peut - nous pouvons - vous pouvez - ils peuvent.

Vouloir (to want) : je veux - tu veux - il veut - nous voulons - vous voulez - ils veulent.

Faire (to do) : je fais - tu fais - il fait - nous faisons - vous faites - ils font.

EXERCISES

1. Replace «tu» with «vous».

Tu aimes Laure ? → *Vous aimez Laure ?*

Tu viens souvent dans ce café ?
Tu connais beaucoup de gens ?
Es-tu vraiment amoureuse d'Étienne ?
Tu sors toujours avec Marie ?

2. Replace «vous» with «tu».

Vous lui plaisez beaucoup. Vous êtes marié(e) ? Vous connaissez mon mari ? Vous accompagnez votre femme ?

3. Conjugate the verbs in brackets in the present tense.

Il *(vouloir)* absolument le voir. Je ne *(pouvoir)* pas le supporter. Ce garçon lui *(faire)* du mal. Ses amis *(pouvoir)* l'apprécier.

KEY TO EXERCISES

1. Vous venez... - Vous connaissez... - Êtes-vous... - Vous sortez...
2. Tu lui plais... - Tu es... - Tu connais... - Tu accompagnes ta femme ?
3. veut - peux - fait - peuvent.

HOW TO SAY IT !

DÉCLARER SES SENTIMENTS :

– Je t'aime. Je l'adore.
– J'en suis folle.
– Tu me fais craquer.
– Il m'énerve.
– Elle m'agace. Je te déteste.
– Je ne le supporte pas.
– Je ne peux pas la voir.

EXPRESSING ONE'S FEELINGS :

– I love you. I adore him/her.
– I'm crazy about him/her/it.
– You make me lose control.
– He gets on my nerves.
– She annoys me. I hate you.
– I can't stand him.
– I can't stand her.

JUGER QUELQU'UN :

– Il/elle est pas mal.
– Il/elle est sympa/génial(e) /brillant(e)...
– Il/elle est pénible, ennuyeux(se), assommant(e)...

JUDGING SOMEONE :

– He/she isn't bad.
– He/she's nice/tremendous/ brilliant...
– He/she's a pain, boring, deadly dull...

It was love at first sight !
(coup de foudre = bolt of lightning / love at first sight)

« L'an dernier, nous avons trouvé dans la rue un petit chien qui semblait perdu. Nous lui avons donné à boire et il n'a plus voulu partir de la maison. Nous avons tout de même contacté la Société protectrice des animaux (S.P.A.) et fait paraître une annonce dans le journal, sans résultat. Bref, nous l'avons adopté, et emmené chez le vétérinaire pour le faire vacciner. Et notre chat a dû accepter de partager son territoire ! »

« Last year we found a little dog who seemed lost in the street. We gave him a drink and (after that) he wouldn't leave the house. All the same, we contacted the Society for the Protection of Animals (S.P.A.) and placed an advert in the newspaper, without any result. So, we adopted him and took him to the vet to get him vaccinated. And our cat had to agree to share his territory ! »

BON À SAVOIR

With its 9 million dogs and 6 million cats, France boasts more pets than any other country in Europe! Strict regulations govern the presence of animals in public places - mainly in parks and gardens, where dogs are simply forbidden or must be kept on a leash, and on public transport (bus, underground, train) where cats must be carried in specially-designed baskets.
Enquire whether pets are allowed in the hotels and restaurants you intend to visit.
Hunting divides the French into those who bitterly oppose the sport and those who strongly support it. Certain traditional forms of hunting such as "la chasse à la palombe" (woodpigeon hunting) in South-West France, "la chasse à courre" (hunting without weapons, using dogs) and "la chasse aux renards" (fox hunting) are subject to intense debate. The same is true of "les corridas" (bullfights) in the south of France.

VOCABULARY

un vétérinaire	veterinary surgeon
un animal	animal
une bête	animal, creature
un chat	cat
un chien	dog
un poisson (rouge)	fish (goldfish)
un aquarium	aquarium
une cage	cage
une ferme	farm
une laisse	leash
un pedigree	pedigree
une plume	feather
le poil	hair, coat (animal)
domestiqué	domesticated,tame
(de) race	breed (purebred)
sauvage	wild
un vaccin	vaccine
un zoo	zoo
aboyer	to bark
apprivoiser	to tame
caresser	to stroke
dresser	to train
miauler	to mew
ronronner	to purr

GRAMMAR

▌ *The perfect and the imperfect :*

The perfect and the imperfect are both past tenses.

The perfect tense describes a single completed action which interrupts another one already under way, described by the imperfect.

– *Tu as vu ce que faisait le chien ?*
– *Il aboyait quand je suis entré(e).*

▌ *An irregular verb :* «devoir» *(= to have to/be obliged) :*

– **Present indicative :** je dois - nous devons - ils doivent.
– **Future :** je devrai - tu devras - ils devront.
– **Imperfect :** je devais - tu devais - nous devions.
– **Perfect :** j'ai dû - tu as dû - ils ont dû.

EXERCISES

1. Conjugate the verbs in the imperfect or the perfect.

L'oiseau *(chanter)* quand on *(ouvrir)* sa cage.
Il *(faire)* du cheval quand je l'*(rencontrer)*.
Elle *(caresser)* le chat quand tu *(rentrer)*.
Cette bête *(être)* sauvage mais on l'*(apprivoiser)*.

2. Put into the imperfect.

Ils doivent l'adopter. → Ils devaient l'adopter.

Il l'emmène chez le vétérinaire. Je le promène. On le vaccine.

3. Translate.

Il y a trop de poissons dans l'aquarium. Quand j'étais jeune, j'habitais à la campagne. Les animaux doivent être tenus en laisse.

KEY TO EXERCISES

1. chantait / a ouvert – faisait / ai rencontré. – caressait / es rentré(e) – était / a apprivoisée.
2. Il l'emmenait... – Je le promenais. – On le vaccinait.
3. There are too many fish in the aquarium. When I was young I lived in the country. Animals must be kept on a leash.

HOW TO SAY IT !

PARLER DE SES CRAINTES :	**EXPRESSING ONE'S FEARS :**
– J'ai peur qu'il n'aboie.	*– I'm frightened that it'll bark.*
– Je crains fort qu'il ne soit malade.	*– I seriously fear that he may be ill.*
– Il se pourrait bien qu'il s'échappe.	*– He might well escape.*
– Je sens que ça se passera mal.	*– I feel that it will go badly.*
– Ça va mal se passer !	*– It's going to go badly!*

PARLER DE SES ESPOIRS :	**EXPRESSING ONE'S HOPES :**
– J'espère que ça ira.	*– I hope it will be alright.*
– J'aimerais bien que ça marche.	*– I'd really like it to work.*
– Ça devrait bien se passer.	*– It should come off okay.*
– Ça doit bien marcher !	*– It should work well.*
– Pas de problèmes, ça marchera.	*– No problem. It'll work.*

This dog's well trained !
(dresser = to train / stand up)

Argent

– J'aimerais acheter cette table, combien coûte-t-elle ?
– 19 500 francs.
– C'est un peu cher !
– Elle est ancienne. C'est un modèle unique.
– Par hasard, vous n'envisagez pas de faire des soldes sur ces articles ?
– C'est totalement impossible, mais vous avez là un excellent rapport qualité/prix. Si ça vous intéresse, on peut vous proposer des facilités de paiement.

– I'd like to buy this table. How much does it cost ?
– 19,500 francs.
– It's a bit expensive !
– It's old. It's the only one of its kind.
– You're not planning, by any chance, to make reductions on these articles ?
– It's completely out of the question, but it's outstanding quality for the price. If you're interested, we can offer you easy terms of payment.

Prices are not controlled in France except for certain products and services: gas, electricity, telephone, tickets on public transport (SNCF, metro ...)

French people have their salaries paid directly into a current account at a bank or post office ("compte courant bancaire ou postal").

Cheques are a means of payment widely used by companies and individuals although credit cards (that are also known as "carte bleue (CB)") are increasingly used by individuals to settle their purchases or withdraw money from cash dispensers ("distributeurs de billets") in the street, stations, airports ...

If you want to withdraw cash over the counter at a post office or a bank, you will be asked to produce proof of your identity.

VOCABULARY

une affaire	deal, bargain
un bénéfice	profit
un gain	gain, earnings
un paiement	payment
- comptant	- in cash
- à crédit	- on credit
- en liquide	- in cash
une carte (bancaire)	(banker's) card
une perte	loss
un pourcentage	percentage
un prix	price
un rabais	discount
une réduction	reduction
une vente	sale
un client	customer
un commerçant	shopkeeper
augmenter	to increase
baisser	to drop
échanger	to exchange
marchander	to bargain over
payer	to pay
régler	to settle
rembourser	to repay
vendre	to sell

GRAMMAR

- **Articles :**
  - ***Definite articles :***
    masculine singular : *le* *prix*
    feminine singular : *la* *réduction*
    plural : *les* *soldes.*
  - ***Indefinite articles :***
    masculine singular : *un* *article*
    feminine singular : *une* *affaire*
    plural : *des* *achats.*
- ***Some indefinite pronouns :***

tout (toute, tous, toutes) (all), **(pas) un** (not one), **aucun(e)** (none), **rien** (nothing), **autre** (other), **quelqu'un** (someone), **nul** (nobody), **personne** (nobody), **certain(e)(s)** (certain), **plusieurs** (several) ...

EXERCISES

1. Use the appropriate indefinite pronoun to change these sentences into their opposites.

tout - tous - aucun(e)

Quelqu'un est venu. → Personne n'est venu.

Toutes les banques sont fermées. Pas un intérêt n'a baissé. Nul ne comprend les mouvements de l'épargne.

2. Complete the following.

... clients font la queue au guichet. Donnez-moi ... ce que vous voulez. Ah ! c'est ... employée du magasin. ... est écrit dans cet agenda.

3. Complete with an appropriate indefinite article or pronoun.

Ils ont pris des billets de loterie mais ... n'a gagné. Voilà ... livre de comptes. ... musiciens donneront un concert ce soir. ... n'est venu aujourd'hui.

KEY TO EXERCISES

1. Aucune banque n'est fermée. Tous les intérêts ont baissé. Tout le monde comprend les mouvements de l'épargne.
2. les/des - tout - une - tout.
3. aucun/personne - un - des - personne/nul.

HOW TO SAY IT !

Demander un prix :

– Je voudrais connaître le prix.
– Cet article vaut combien ?
– Ça coûte combien ?
– Quel est le prix ?
– C'est le montant exact ?

Asking for a price :

– I'd like to know the price.
– How much is this article ?
– How much does it cost ?
– What's the price ?
– What's the exact amount ?

Demander un rabais :

– C'est un peu trop cher !
– Vous faites 30 % sur ces articles ?
– Vous me le laissez à combien ?
– C'est combien ?
– Vous en demandez combien ?

– Faites-moi un prix.
– Vous faites une réduction ?

Asking for a reduction :

– It's a little too expensive !
– Do you give a 30% reduction on these articles ?
– You'll let me have it for how much ?
– How much is it ?
– How much are you asking for it ?
– Give me a reduction.
– Will you give a reduction ?

You've been taken for a ride.
(se faire avoir = to be « had »)

Vernissage à la Galerie Moug

C'est avec un grand succès que l'exposition du peintre Zilda a été inaugurée hier dans notre ville.

L'artiste y a présenté une grande variété de tableaux : de la peinture la plus intimiste à des œuvres plus abstraites. Il a aussi exposé quelques sculptures étonnantes, rappelant l'art africain. .

Nous encourageons vivement nos lecteurs à s'y rendre.

L'exposition est ouverte tous les jours, sauf le mardi, de 10 heures à 18 heures sans interruption.

G. L. ■

Preview at the Galerie Moug

Yesterday's inauguration in our town of the exhibition of the painter Zilda was a great success.

The artist has included a wide variety of pictures ranging from painting of the most intimist kind to more abstract works. He has also exhibited a few surprising sculptures reminiscent of African art.

We strongly advise our readers to visit it.

The exhibition is open every day except Tuesdays, from 10 a.m. until 6 p.m., without interruption.

G. L. ■

BON À SAVOIR

If you want to know what cultural or artistic events are being organised in the part of France you happen to be visiting, you can get a lot of details from guidebooks or the tourist office, but the local press and posters in the street are another valuable source of information! Special magazines list cultural events in Paris

You usually need a personal invitation to attend the "première" (first night) of a new show or the "vernissage" (preview) of an exhibition.

The most popular places in Paris from a cultural point of view are the Georges-Pompidou centre of modern art (known as "le Centre Beaubourg" after the name of the "quartier" in which it is built), the "cité de La Villette" (centre for science and industry) and the Louvre, Orsay and Picasso museums.

Every year, Paris welcomes the "Foire internationale d'art contemporain" (international modern art exhibition) where you can see works from the most prestigious art galleries worldwide.

VOCABULARY

le dessin	drawing
la peinture	painting
la sculpture	sculpture
l'architecture	architecture
la chanson	song
la danse	dance
les variétés	variety show
un musée	museum
l'opéra	opera
une galerie	gallery
un(e) artiste	artist
un(e) chanteur(euse)	singer
un écrivain	writer
un peintre	painter
un photographe	photographer
une entrée	entry, entrance
une exposition	exhibition
la fermeture	closure
l'ouverture	opening
une réduction	reduction
la sortie	exit
abstrait	abstract
classique	classical
moderne	modern

GRAMMAR

▮ *Agreement of adjectives :*

Adjectives ending in a silent consonant take an « e » in the feminine and the consonant is pronounced

*grand → grand**e***　　*clos → clos**e***
*petit → petit**e***　　*cher → chèr**e***

Other adjectives change their form :

*brésilien → brésilien**ne***　　*bon → bon**ne***

▮ *The superlative :*

- **relative :** definite article + **plus/moins**.
  L'architecture la moins classique.
- **absolute : très**.
  *Un style **très** expressif.*

EXERCISES

1. Put into the feminine form.

Il est rond. → Elle est ronde.

Vous êtes lents. Tu es américain. Ils sont bruns. Il est peint à la main. Tu es divin.

2. Introduce the superlative into the following sentences.

La *Joconde* est une peinture célèbre de Leonard de Vinci. Le Louvre est un grand musée de Paris. C'est un sculpteur inconnu.

3. Translate.

À quelle heure ouvre le musée ? Je n'aime pas ces peintures. Il y a des tarifs réduits dans tous les musées. On ne paie pas pour visiter les galeries.

KEY TO EXERCISES

1. Vous êtes lentes. Tu es américaine. Elles sont brunes. Elle est peinte à la main. Tu es divine.
2. La *Joconde* est une peinture très célèbre de Leonard de Vinci. Le Louvre est le plus grand musée de Paris. C'est le sculpteur le moins connu.
3. When does the museum open ? I don't like these paintings. There are reduced rates in all the museums. You don't pay to visit the galleries.

HOW TO SAY IT !

ENCOURAGER :

– Nous vous encourageons à continuer.
– Allez-y. Vas-y. Allez !
– N'hésite pas !
– Vous devriez poursuivre votre effort.

ENCOURAGING :

– We encourage you to continue.
– Go on !
– Don't hesitate.
– You should keep up your effort.

EXPRIMER L'ADMIRATION :

– C'est/je trouve que c'est admirable/fantastique/magnifique/remarquable/superbe.
– Que c'est beau !
– Qu'est-ce qu'elle est belle !
– Comme c'est bien fait !

EXPRESSING ADMIRATION :

– It's/I find it admirable/fantastic/magnificent/remarkable/superb ...
– How beautiful/attractive it is !
– How beautiful she/it is !
– How well made it is !

What a crude painting !
(croûte = crust / unskilful painting)

M. Manceau/Rapho

Aéroport de Roissy.

Formalities

A passport or identity card is enough if you are a citizen of an EEC-member state. Other nationalities should obtain a visa from the French consulate in their country.

Americans, Canadians, Japanese and all nationals from countries belonging to the Council of Europe (Sweden, Norway, for example) with the exception of Turkey, are not required to obtain visas but must show a valid passport.

Note that if you stay in France for more than three months, you will have to obtain a residence permit ("carte de séjour").

Customs quotas for EEC nationals are as follows : 300 cigarettes ; 3 litres of wine and spirits less than 22° alcohol, 1.5 litres of spirits more than 22°, and duty-free goods ("marchandise en franchise") not exceeding the equivalent of FF2800.

Transport

If you arrive in Paris by train, the different mainline stations are all fairly central and connected by a fast and frequent underground train service (the famous Paris "métro").

If you are travelling by 'plane, you may arrive at one of two airports :

Roissy Charles de Gaulle, terminal 1 or 2 (tel. : (33) 1 48 62 12 12) to the north-east of Paris, or *Orly* airport, two terminals : "sud" and "ouest" (tel. : (33) 1 49 75 52 52), to the south of Paris.

You have a choice of taxis, trains and buses to get to Paris from the airport. **Taxis** from both airports will charge you about FF250 (1991 rates). It is easy to take the **train** (or rather the **RER**, "réseau express régional" - fast urban train service) from Roissy. A free shuttle service will take you from the airport to the station. The RER serves Paris and the suburbs, so get off the train at the "Gare du Nord" or (better) at "Châtelet" in central Paris.

There is also a frequent bus service : the Air France shuttle will take you to l'étoile (Arc de Triomphe) *from Roissy* and to Les Invalides *from Orly*. An alternative bus service from Orly ("Orlybus") will take you to Denfert Rochereau.

In the provinces : you have a choice between taxis (expect to pay about the same as in Paris) and a shuttle service.

Bar

– Bonjour monsieur, vous désirez ?
– Eh bien ! J'aimerais un demi pour commencer.
– ... Un demi ! et avec ça ?
– Qu'est-ce que vous avez à manger ?
– Salades, omelettes, le plat du jour...
– Vous n'avez pas de croque-monsieur ?
– Non, mais on a des sandwiches.
– Des sandwiches à quoi ?
– Jambon, pâté, saucisson, rillettes, fromage...
– Ce sera un sandwich au jambon.
– Ça marche !
– Ah... s'il vous plaît ! Je suis pressé. Vous pourriez m'apporter un café et l'addition en même temps ?
– Bien sûr !

– Good morning, sir. What would you like ?
– Well, I'd like a half (of beer) to start with.
– ... A half. Anything else ?
– What have you got to eat ?
– Salads, omelettes, today's special ...
– You don't have any toasted cheese sandwiches with ham ?
– No, but we have ordinary sandwiches.
– What kind of sandwiches ?
– Ham, pâté, sausage, rillettes (potted pork), cheese ...
– Bring me a ham sandwich.
– Righto, sir !
– Oh ... excuse me ! I'm in a hurry. Could you bring me a coffee and the bill at the same time ?
– Certainly.

BON À SAVOIR

There are innumerable cafés and bars in France, and an immense number of "brasseries" and "bistrots" (something between a café and a pub). These are the places where people meet to talk, to pass the time of day, relax, read, watch the passers-by ... especially in the summer, when a lot of cafés put tables and chairs out on the pavement ("en terrasse").
Among the more famous cafés in Paris, we could mention "Le Café de Flore", "Les Deux-Magots", "La Coupole"...
Patrons usually have a choice of simple dishes (including a "plat du jour" or the special dish of the day) and relatively quick service.
Some cafés, identified by a red diamond, known as "tabacs", also sell cigarettes, postage stamps, postcards, etc...

VOCABULARY

une bière	beer	**une terrasse**	pavement area
un café	café, coffee	**les toilettes**	toilet
un (café) crème	white coffee	**le garçon**	waiter
une carafe	carafe, decanter	**le patron**	proprietor
un croque-monsieur	toasted cheese sandwich with ham	**un serveur**	waiter, barman
		l'addition	bill
un demi	half (of beer)	**un pourboire**	tip
un express	espresso (coffee)	**une table**	table
du pain	bread	**choisir**	to choose
du thé	tea	**demander**	to ask for
du vin	wine	**manger**	to eat
un bistrot	café, pub	**servir**	to serve
un comptoir	bar, counter	**vouloir**	to want

GRAMMAR

The future :

- **For « -er » verbs :** Simply take the infinitive and add the endings of the future tense **(-ai, -as, -a, -ons, -ez, -ont)**
  Manger : *manger**ai/as/a/ons/ez/ont***
  ▲ **Aller :** *j'irai, tu iras, il ira, nous irons, vous irez, ils iront.*
- **For « -ir » verbs :** again simply add the endings of the future tense to the infinitive : *J'offrirai ... Ils ouvriront.*
- **For « -re » verbs :** take the infinitive - e **+ -ai, -as, -a, -ons, -ez, -ont**. *Je prendrai.* (prendre)

The conditional :

The conditional mood describes what would happen if something else were to happen. The stem of the verb is the same as the one used to form the future and displays the same irregularities. The conditional is formed using the following endings : **-ais, -ais, -ait, -ions, -iez, -aient**.
Je commanderais... Il/Elle voudrait...

EXERCISES

1. Put the following sentences into the future.

Je lui paie un café. → *Je lui paierai un café.*

Tu aimes la bière. On se retrouve à quel café ? Nous proposons des sandwiches en tout genre. Après le sandwich vous voulez autre chose ?

2. Put the verb in brackets into the appropriate form of the conditional :

Si j'avais de l'argent, je (prendre) autre chose. Si le serveur était plus rapide, tu (pouvoir) demander l'addition. S'il nous donnait rendez-vous, ce (être) en terrasse. Si on en avait les moyens, on (aller) plus souvent au café.

3. Choose between the future and the conditional :

J'(aimer) un café, s'il vous plaît. Dis-lui que je (prendre) un jus d'orange. S'il y avait moins de bruit, tu (étudier) au café. Pour moi, ce (être) un express. Je (être) au bistrot dans une heure, attends-moi !

KEY TO EXERCISES

1. aimeras – retrouvera – proposerons – voudrez.
2. prendrais – pourrais – serait – irait.
3. aimerais – prendrai – étudierais – sera – serai.

HOW TO SAY IT !

LE SERVEUR S'ADRESSE AU CLIENT :

– Vous désirez ?
– Je vous sers ?
– Qu'est-ce que je vous sers ?

– Oui ?
– Et pour vous ?

THE WAITER ADRESSING THE CUSTOMER :

– What would you like ?
– May I serve you ?
– What would you like me to bring you ?
– Yes ?
– And for you ?

POUR S'ADRESSER AU SERVEUR, À LA SERVEUSE :

– S'il vous plaît !
– Monsieur ! / Madame !
– Je voudrais un café.
– J'aimerais déjeuner.
– Apportez-moi la carte, s'il vous plaît.
– Donnez-moi l'addition.

ADRESSING THE WAITER, WAITRESS :

– Excuse me !
– Waiter ! / Waitress !
– I'd like a coffee.
– I'd like to have lunch.
– Bring me the menu, please.

– Give me the bill.

Shall we have a drink ?
(pot = pot, jar / drink)

– Alors, Henri, que penses-tu de la conjoncture économique ?
– À court terme, la situation est difficile à évaluer, mais à long terme, elle n'est peut-être pas mauvaise.
– Tu es inquiet pour les actions ou pour les obligations ?
– Oh ! Je pense surtout aux valeurs étrangères. Les périodes de tension politique ne sont pas bonnes pour la Bourse.
– C'est vrai, regarde les investisseurs : ils sont prudents et les marchés restent très peu actifs.
– Ne perdons quand même pas notre optimisme...
– Écoute, la Bourse est un peu comme le temps : elle change souvent !

– Well, Henri, what do you think of the economic situation ?
– In the short term, it's difficult to judge, but it's not bad in the long term, perhaps.
– Are you worried about stocks or bonds ?
– Oh, I'm mainly concerned about foreign securities. Periods of political tension aren't good for the stock market
– That's true, look at the investors : they're being cautious and the markets are rather sluggish.
– But let's not be pessimistic...
– Well, the stock market is a bit like the weather : it changes all the time.

BON À SAVOIR

When people in France talk about the stock market, they are probably thinking about Paris where most deals are made.

But it isn't essential to go to the Paris Stock Exchange (Palais Brongniart) to find out about the financial market. Investors can obtain ample information about the state of the market in France (SICAV or unit trusts, the CAC 40 stock market index ...) and abroad (Dow Jones index, foreign exchange rates ...) from the radio, television, newspapers, Minitel and the banks. "La Tribune de l'Expansion" and "Les Echos" are two important financial newspapers, but the leading dailies (such as "Le Monde" and "Le Figaro") also publish the latest Stock Market prices.

VOCABULARY

une action	share
la baisse	decline
un bénéfice	profit
la conjoncture	situation, climate
le crédit	credit
l'économie	economy
la hausse	rise
un indice	index
un investissement	investment
une obligation	bond
une perspective	outlook
une plus-value	capital gain
un pourcentage	percentage
une tension	tension
le terme	term, deadline
une valeur	value
un agent de change	stockbroker
un cadre	executive
un homme d'affaires	businessman
coter	to quote, list
emporter	to take away
gagner	to gain, earn
vendre	to sell
stable	stable

GRAMMAR

The negative imperative :

The imperative has only three persons : **tu, nous, vous.**
The subject pronouns are not used in the imperative :
Écoute les informations ! Sois patient !
The negative imperative is usually constructed as follows :
ne + verb + pas.
Ne perdons pas notre optimisme !

The verb **«être inquiet»** :
Ne sois pas inquiet !
Ne soyons pas inquiets !
Ne soyez pas inquiet(s) !

The verb **«investir»** :
N'investis pas !
N'investissons pas !
N'investissez pas !

EXERCISES

1. Put the verbs into the imperative.

Mesdames, messieurs, *(ne pas fumer)*, s'il vous plaît.
(Finir) vite ce travail, après vous serez payés.
(Être) raisonnables si nous voulons emporter cette affaire.
(Lire) «les Échos» si tu veux tout savoir sur l'économie.

2. Choose the appropriate verb and put it into the imperative.

Être – avoir – prendre – se servir.
..... vos dossiers avant d'aller à la réunion. .....-vous ! ..... confiance en nous, tu verras ! ..... aimable avec tes clients !

3. Transform the sentences into the negative imperative.

Vous regardez la Bourse à la télévision. → Ne regardez pas la Bourse à la télévision !
Tu achètes des actions aujourd'hui. Nous allons à la Bourse. Vous finissez vos comptes. Vous êtes trop prudents dans vos investissements. Nous avons confiance dans ces valeurs.

KEY TO EXERCISES

1. ne fumez pas – Finissez – Soyons – Lis.
2. Prenez – Servez – Aie – Sois.
3. N'achète pas d'actions aujourd'hui. N'allons pas à la Bourse. Ne finissez pas vos comptes. Ne soyez pas trop prudents dans vos investissements. N'ayons pas confiance dans ces valeurs.

HOW TO SAY IT !

DONNER SON OPINION, DIRE SON AVIS :

– À mon avis, la Bourse va encore monter.
– Selon moi, les valeurs étrangères progresseront à la hausse.
– Je pense qu'il faut acheter des actions.
– Je suis (presque) certain(e) que les obligations vont baisser.
– Il me semble que l'indice CAC 40 est stable.

EXPRESSING ONE'S OPINION, POINT OF VIEW :

– In my opinion, the stock market's going to go up again.
– According to me, foreign securities will continue to rise.
– I think I (you, he, etc.) should buy some shares.
– I'm (almost) sure that bonds are going to fall.
– It seems to me that the CAC 40 index is stable.

Take care of the pennies and the pounds will take care of themselves.
(lit. "There are no small savings")

Centre-ville

Si tu veux visiter la ville, je te conseille d'y aller à pied ou en bus.

Tu sais, il y a beaucoup de circulation et les embouteillages sont fréquents dans le centre.

Comme ça tu éviteras les problèmes de stationnement et les mauvaises surprises : tous les parkings sont payants ; dans les rues, les places pour se garer sont rares, le temps est limité à 2 heures maximum et tu risques une amende ou la fourrière !

Ça m'est arrivé le mois dernier !

Et en plus, le bus B t'amène en plein centre-ville : tu descends à l'arrêt « Cathédrale », et de là, tu rejoins les rues piétonnes.

C'est bien indiqué.

If you want to visit the town, I advise you to go on foot or by bus.
There's a lot of traffic, you know, and there are often traffic jams in the centre.
That way you'll avoid parking problems and unpleasant surprises ; there's a charge for all the car parks ; there are very few parking places in the street, parking time is limited to 2 hours maximum and you run the risk of a fine or the car pound.
That happened to me last month !
And what's more, the bus B takes you right to the town centre : you get off at the Cathedral stop and from there you can get to the pedestrian precinct.
It's well sign-posted.

Town centre

An increasing number of towns and cities in France are transforming their centres into pedestrian precincts ("quartiers piétonniers") and everything is done to discourage motorists.

On-street parking is allowed only for limited periods of time: a ticket must be taken from the machine and placed inside the car, against the windscreen (it must be visible from the outside).

Generally speaking, a charge is made for parking between 9 a.m. and 7 p.m. every day of the week except Sundays and bank holidays.

VOCABULARY

un chemin	path, way, road	**avant**	before
une direction	direction	**(à) côté**	next to
un pont	bridge	**derrière**	behind
un trottoir	pavement	**devant**	in front of
une carte	map	**en face**	opposite
un guide	guide, guidebook	**loin**	far
une pancarte	(road)sign	**tout droit**	straight ahead
un panneau	signpost	**chercher**	to look for
un plan	(street) map, plan	**filer**	to dash (past)
un point de repère	landmark	**passer**	to go past
		(se) perdre	to get lost
une signalisation	roadsigns	**signaler**	to signal
après	after	**suivre**	to follow

Centre-ville

GRAMMAR

■ *The passive :*

In the passive form of the verb, the subject undergoes the action.

• The passive is formed with the verb « **être** » and the appropriate form of the past participle of the verb.

L'orage détruit les routes. → Les routes sont détruites par l'orage.
(active voice) (passive voice)

• The past participle agrees with the subject of the sentence

Ma voiture a été volée.

EXERCISES

1. Choose the appropriate word.

payant – souterrain – feu – embouteillage.

Arrête-toi, le ..... est rouge. On n'avance pas ! Il y a un ..... . Tu as de l'argent ? Le parking est ..... . Prends le passage ..... pour traverser.

2. Change into the passive form as shown in the example.

On autorise le stationnement ici. → Le stationnement est autorisé ici.

Les embouteillages te gêneront. On évitera les problèmes. On a modifié le carrefour. On vole des voitures.

3. Change the sentences into the active voice.

Cette ville est visitée par de nombreux touristes.
La circulation est interdite par la police.
Les embouteillages ne sont pas évités par tous les automobilistes.

KEY TO EXERCISES

1. feu – embouteillage – payant – souterrain.
2. Tu seras gêné par les embouteillages. Les problèmes seront évités. Le carrefour a été modifié. Des voitures sont volées.
3. De nombreux touristes visitent cette ville. La police interdit la circulation. Tous les automobilistes n'évitent pas les embouteillages.

HOW TO SAY IT !

COMMENT SUGGÉRER UN MODE DE DÉPLACEMENT :

– Il vaudrait mieux que tu y ailles à pied.
– Vous devriez prendre un taxi.
– Ça serait mieux si on prenait un bus.

HOW TO SUGGEST A MEANS OF TRANSPORT :

– You'd be better off going on foot.
– You should take a taxi.
– It would be better if we took a bus.

COMMENT INTERDIRE :

– On ne doit pas passer au rouge.
– Il ne faut pas traverser maintenant.
– Ne traverse pas !
– Interdiction de traverser ici !
– Il est interdit de stationner là !

PROHIBITING SOMETHING :

– You mustn't go when the lights are red.
– You mustn't cross now.
– Don't cross !
– No crossing here !
– Parking here is prohibited !

I jumped the traffic light again !
(griller = to grill, roast)

– Quel retour de vacances ! Hier, en sortant de l'autoroute du Sud, au péage, on allait payer quand une voiture qui nous suivait nous a heurtés : pare-chocs, coffre et feux arrière complètement enfoncés !
On s'est arrêtés sur le parking pour remplir le constat à l'amiable... ensuite il a fallu trouver un garage ouvert – il était 18 h 30 !
Heureusement, le mécanicien nous a dit qu'on pouvait reprendre la route malgré les dégâts : les roues et le moteur lui ont paru en bon état.
On a roulé lentement, et on est finalement arrivé à la maison à minuit, tous épuisés !

- What a journey back from the holiday ! Yesterday, as we were leaving the South motorway, we were just about to pay at the tollgate, when we were hit by a car which was following us : bumper, boot and rear lights completely smashed in !
We stopped in the parking area to fill out the accident report .... then we had to find a garage that was open - it was 6.30 in the evening !
Fortunately, the mechanic told us that we could continue our journey despite the damage : the wheels and the engine seemed to him to be in good order.
We drove slowly, and finally arrived home at midnight ; we were all exhausted !

You must pay to use most French motorways (only certain short sections are free).
The speed limit is 130 kilometres per hour (km/hr) on motorways, 90 km/hr on other roads and 50 km/hr in built-up areas - about 80, 55 and 30 m.p.h. respectively. (It's easy to convert miles into kilometres and vice-versa if you remember that 80 km = 50 miles).
Exceeding the speed limit is punishable by fine and by loss of licence (for varying lengths of time).
All motor vehicles must be insured. In the event of an accident, each driver must fill in a report describing the circumstances of the accident and each driver's share of responsibility. This accident report is then sent to the insurance company which appoints a valuer to determine the amount of damage (in a garage approved by the insurance company).

VOCABULARY

une route	road
une déviation	diversion
un panneau	signpost
un radar	radar
la signalisation	signposting
une ambulance	ambulance
un constat	(accident) report
une crevaison	puncture
des dégâts	damage
une panne	breakdown
un dépannage	fixing (a breakdown)
une réparation	repair
un mécanicien	mechanic
la mécanique	mechanics
le niveau	level
un pneu	tyre
grave	serious
vite	fast
(s')arrêter	to stop
conduire	to drive
doubler	to overtake
freiner	to brake
ralentir	to slow down
rouler	to go, run (of a car)

GRAMMAR

The perfect tense :

The perfect tense is a past tense.

• It is constructed with « **avoir** » conjugated in the present + the past participle of the verb.
Elle a conduit. Elles ont conduit.

• It is constructed with « **être** » conjugated in the present + the past participle of the verb.
Elle est partie. Ils sont venus.

• The auxiliary « **être** » is used :
– to conjugate reflexive verbs (se lever...),
– to form the passive voice,
– to conjugate verbs expressing movement or state *(aller, entrer, sortir, venir...).*

EXERCISES

1. *Choose the appropriate word.*

doubler – vitesse – vite – péage.

Ne roule pas trop ..... . Tu peux ..... , il n'y a personne sur la route. La ... est limitée à 60 km/h ici. En France, les autoroutes sont à ..... .

2. *Choose the correct form of the perfect tense (with « avoir » or « être »).*

Elle (être) accidentée. Est-ce que tu (voir) cette voiture ? J' (trouver) un bon garage. Vous (vérifier) les pneus ?

3. *Transform as shown in the example, using the perfect tense. (Remember to choose the right auxiliary !)*

Vous partez en voiture ? → Vous êtes parti(e-s-es) en voiture ?

Il vient dès que possible. Nous roulons toute la nuit. Je m'arrête au péage. Les ambulances arrivent vite.

KEY TO EXERCISES

1. vite – doubler – vitesse – péage.
2. a été – as vu – ai trouvé – avez vérifié.
3. Il est venu dès que possible. Nous avons roulé toute la nuit. Je me suis arrêté(e) au péage. Les ambulances sont arrivées vite.

HOW TO SAY IT !

DEMANDER UN SERVICE OU DE L'AIDE :

– Je suis en panne, vous pourriez m'aider ?
– Pourriez-vous me dépanner ?
– Vous pouvez me donner un coup de main ?
– Est-ce que vous pouvez me sortir de là ?

REQUESTING A SERVICE OR ASSISTANCE :

– I've broken down, could you help me ?
– Could you help me out ?
– Can you give me a hand ?
– Can you get me out of this ?

DONNER DES CONSIGNES :

– Vous vérifiez les niveaux, s'il vous plaît ?
– Vous me faites le plein ?
– Le plein, s'il vous plaît !
– Rangez votre véhicule !
– Veuillez arrêter votre moteur, s'il vous plaît.

GIVING ORDERS :

– Could you check the levels, please ?
– Could you fill it up, please ?
– Fill it up, please !
– Park your car !
– Would you stop your engine, please.

I rolled the car twice, darling !
(tonneau = barrel / somersault)

Coiffeur

– Bonjour !
– Bonjour, madame ! Qu'est-ce qu'on vous fait aujourd'hui ?
– Je voudrais une coupe avec la nuque bien dégagée, pour l'été.
– Pas de problème, je vais vous faire ça. Après le shampooing, je vous mets une crème ? Vous avez les cheveux secs, ça leur fera du bien !
– D'accord, je crois que j'aimerais bien aussi une permanente légère pour leur donner du volume, et quelque chose pour les éclaircir. Ils sont trop ternes en ce moment.
– Très bien. Alors, allons-y !

– Good morning !
– Good morning, Madam ! What can we do for you today ?
– I'd like my hair cut short at the back of the neck, for the summer.
– Certainly, I can do that for you. After the shampoo, shall I put on some conditioner ? You hair's dry ; it will to it good !
– Alright. I think I'd also like a light perm to give it some body, and something to brighten it. It's too dull at the moment.
– Very well. Let's make a start then !

Hairdresser

BON À SAVOIR

Hairdressing salons may specialise in lady's hairdressing ("salon de coiffure pour dames") or in gentlemen's hairdressing ("salon de coiffure pour hommes") but more frequently cater for both ladies and gentlemen ("masculin/féminin"). Prices can vary considerably from one hairdresser's to the next so before going in, don't forget to consult the price list which should, by law, be posted up in the window.
Some famous "coiffeurs" such as Maniatis or Alexandre export their styles worldwide. Others run schools and "ateliers" (literally : workshops) throughout France : Jean-Louis David, Dessange, Harlow...
Perfume shops and beauty parlours are often combined into one shop. They offer a range of services : epilation, face-care, Ultra Violet radiation (for tanning) and massages (for slimming)...

VOCABULARY

un(e) coiffeur(euse)	hairdresser
une manucure	manicurist
un salon de coiffure	hairdressing salon
un brushing	blow-dry
une brosse	brush
les ciseaux	scissors
un peigne	comb
un rasoir	razor
un sèche-cheveux	hair-drier
un dégradé	layering
(du) gel	gel
une barbe	beard
une moustache	moustache
court	short
frisé	curly
long	long
raide	straight
coiffer	to do sb's hair
démêler	to untangle
laver	to wash
raser	to shave
rincer	to rinse
sécher	to dry
teindre	to dye
couper	to cut

GRAMMAR

- ***The verb «avoir» in the present indicative :***
  J'ai - tu as - il a - nous avons - vous avez - ils ont.
- ***The interrogative form :***
  (rising intonation) *Tu vas chez le coiffeur ?*
  (inversion of the subject) *Veux-tu venir avec nous ?*
  (*Qu'est-ce que* + normal order) *Qu'est-ce que tu fais ?*

EXERCISES

1. Choose the appropriate word.

peigne - coupe - ciseaux - rasoir

Elle a une ..... superbe.
Prends ce ..... pour te coiffer.
Il utilise toujours un ..... électrique.
Ces ..... coupent mal.

2. Complete the following sentences using the present tense of «avoir».

Ils ..... de la chance.
On ..... tout ici.
Il n'y ..... plus rien.
Vous ..... une belle permanente.

3. Transform the following questions, as in the example.

Je prends ce shampooing, et toi ? → Qu'est-ce que tu prends ?

Il met du gel, et elle ?
Elle a fait un dégradé, et lui ?
J'ai pris les ciseaux, et toi ?
J'utilise un rasoir mécanique, et vous ?

KEY TO EXERCISES

1. coupe - peigne - rasoir - ciseaux.
2. ont - a - a - avez.
3. Qu'est-ce qu'elle met ? Qu'est-ce qu'il a fait ? Qu'est-ce que tu as pris ? Qu'est-ce que vous utilisez ?

HOW TO SAY IT !

Comment donner des instructions :

– J'aimerais une coupe plus mode, s'il vous plaît !
– Vous me faites juste une coupe !
– Vous me mettrez aussi un peu de gel !

How to give instructions :

– I'd like a more fashionable haircut, please !
– Just a haircut, please !
– Put a little gel on as well !

Comment décrire quelqu'un :

– Il se laisse pousser la barbe.
– Tu as vu, il perd ses cheveux !
– Il a les cheveux courts et blonds.
– Elle s'est fait friser.

How to describe someone :

– He's letting his beard grow.
– Have you seen, he's losing his hair !
– He has short, blond hair.
– She's had her hair curled.

I prefer the parting on the side!
(raie = parting / ray (fish))

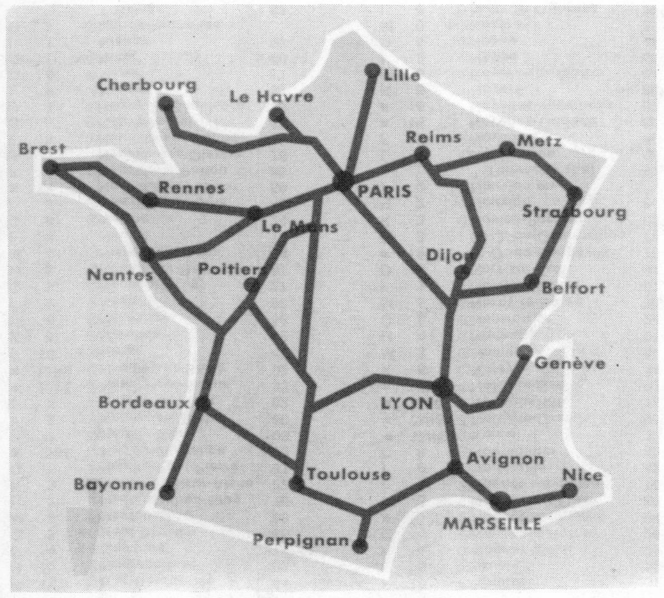

La France routière et touristique

BY PLANE *Make inquiries at your travel agency or at AIR INTER :* 54, rue du Père-Corentin, 75014 Paris, tel : (33) (1) 45 39 25 25.

•

BY TRAIN *In Paris :*
Inquiries : tel : (33) (1) 45 82 50 50
Reservations : tel : (33) (1) 45 85 60 60

BY CAR Useful telephone numbers :
Weather report : (33) (1) 36 65 01 01
CRICR (Regional Centre for Motoring Information and Coordination) : (33) (1) 48 99 33 33.

Preparing your itinerary

• There exists a useful series of road maps published by **Michelin** (scale : 1/200,000) or the French National Geographical Institute (IGN) drawn to three different scales : red collection ("série rouge") - 1/250,000; green collection ("série verte") - 1/100,000; blue collection ("série bleue") - 1/50,000. IGN : 107, avenue de la Boétie, 75008 Paris, tel. : (33) (1) 42 25 87 90.

CAR HIRE ("location de voiture") You must be at least 21 years old and have held a valid driving licence for one year. You may have to present an international driving licence (not if you belong to one of the EEC-member states; your national licence is accepted).
Some useful addresses :
Valem, tel. : (33) (1) 43 55 81 83 / Hertz, tel. : (33) (1) 47 88 51 51
Avis, tel. : (33) (1) 45 50 32 31 / Mattei, tel. : (33) (1) 42 64 48 48
Europcar, tel. : (33) (1) 30 43 82 82 / Citer, tel. : (33) (1) 43 38 15 15.

HITCH-HIKING ("auto-stop") Contact the company Allô Stop Provoya which acts as a clearing house for hitch-hikers and motorists (on the understanding that the costs of the journey are shared).
Allô Stop Provoya : 84, passage Brady, 75010 Paris, tel. : (33) (1) 42 46 00 66 or via Minitel 3615 + COMET.

BY BICYCLE ("en vélo") To hire a bicycle, inquire at a bicycle shop or at any SNCF railway station who will advise.

In Paris : Fédération de cyclotourisme : 8, rue Jean-Marie-Jégo, 75013 Paris, tel. : (33) (1) 45 80 30 21.

ON FOOT ("à pied") There are 40,000 km of paths for hikers and ramblers ("sentiers de grande randonnée" : GR). Buy the IGN map of paths and the corresponding topographical guidebook.

In Paris : Centre d'information sentiers et randonnées : 64, rue de Gergovie, 75014 Paris, tel. : (33) (1) 45 45 31 02.

D'après *Rendez-vous en France,* A. Reboullet, J.-L. Malandain, J. Verdol, Hachette, 1990.

– Je ne comprends vraiment pas ce qui te plaît chez ce garçon.

– Il a de beaux yeux !

– Peut-être, mais il n'y voit rien !

– Eh bien... son sourire me plaît.

– En plus il est presque chauve.

– Là tu exagères ! Il a simplement les cheveux très courts.

– Il est maigre. Et puis t'as vu sa démarche ?

– Ce n'est peut-être pas un athlète mais je le trouve beau comme ça.

– I really don't understand what you like about that boy.
– He's got lovely eyes !
– Perhaps, but he can't see anything.
– Well...I like his smile.
– What's more, he's practically bald.
– You're exaggerating there ! He just has very short hair.
– He's skinny. And have you seen the way he walks ?
– Perhaps he isn't an athlete, but I find him attractive like that.

French people are taking more and more care of their bodies : swimming, jogging, gymnastics, slimming and health courses, sea water therapy ("thalassothérapie"), etc.
The French are not particularly prudish, but naturism is only practised in authorised, "closed" areas.
In the main stations and airports, there are facilities for having "un brin de toilette" – a wash and brush up.
Several myths persist about French hygiene... probably linked to the notion of traditional, unspoilt, rustic France ! The French share the same values of personal hygiene as other developed nations but for questions of such an intimate nature, the reader will have to judge for himself !

VOCABULARY

la tête	head
le crâne	skull
le front	forehead
le nez	nose
les oreilles	ears
la bouche	mouth
les dents	teeth
le visage	face
l'épaule	shoulder
le bras	arm
la main	hand
le doigt	finger
un ongle	fingernail
le dos	back
la poitrine	chest
les poumons	lungs
l'estomac	stomach
la jambe	leg
le genou	knee
le pied	foot
un muscle	muscle
le sexe	genitals, sex
les os	bones
la peau	skin

GRAMMAR

Agreement of adjectives.

• The feminine is usually formed by adding the letter "e" to the masculine form
court/courte ; voisin/voisine. (The final consonant is pronounced in this case.)
joli/jolie ; gai/gaie ; familial/familiale. (No change in pronunciation.)
There is no change when the masculine form already ends in «e»
squelettique

• The letter «s» is added to form the plural
énorme/énormes.
Adjectives already ending in «**s**» or «**x**» do not change.
bas - gros - roux - heureux.

▲ Adjectives ending in **-eau** change to **-eaux :** *beau/beaux.*
▲ Adjectives ending in **-al** change to **-aux :** *normal/normaux.*

EXERCISES

1. Put into the plural.

Elle a un beau corps. → Elles ont de beaux corps.
Il a un bras difforme.
Elle a un sacré mollet !
Pourquoi ta joue est si enflée ?
Il dit que mon genou n'est pas normal.

2. Choose the appropriate adjective.

Il a un (gros/grosse) nez mais des lèvres (fins/fines). J'ai les pieds très (fragile/fragiles). Elle a un (beau/belle) visage.

3. Translate.

Tu as de beaux yeux. Elle a les cheveux blonds. J'ai de grandes oreilles.

KEY TO EXERCISES

1. Ils ont des bras difformes. Elles ont de sacrés mollets ! Pourquoi vos joues sont si enflées ? Ils disent que mes genoux ne sont pas normaux.
2. gros / fines – fragiles – beau.
3. You have beautiful eyes. She has blond hair. I have big ears.

HOW TO SAY IT !

Pour dire son opinion à propos de quelqu'un :

– Oh ! Il a un de ces regards !
– Elle a de ces jambes !
– Quels beaux yeux !
– Elle a une chevelure superbe !
– Il/Elle a du charme !
– Il/Elle est magnifique, beau/belle, pas mal, génial(e)...
– Il/Elle est mignon(ne).
– Il/Elle a un visage ingrat.

– Il/Elle est laid(e), affreux(se), moche [familier].

Expressing an opinion about someone :

– Oh, he's got such a look !
– What legs she's got !
– What beautiful eyes !
– She's got magnificent hair.
– He/she's got charm.
– He/she's magnificent, beautiful, not bad, fantastic....
– He/she's sweet.
– He/she's got an unattractive face.
– He/she's ugly, frightful, ugly (familiar).

What a he-man !
(armoire à glace = wardrobe with a mirror / he-man)

Dates

Jacques : – Quel jour on est ?

Pierre : – Écoute ! En vacances je ne sais jamais.

Jacques : – Il y a bien quelqu'un qui pourra nous renseigner.

Pierre : – Regarde le journal de la dame : mercredi, 15 août.

La dame : – Non, jeune homme, c'est le journal d'avant-hier.

Jacques : – Merci, madame. Alors, on est le vendredi 17 août.

Pierre : – De quelle année ?

Jacques : – Là, tu exagères ! Tu te moques de moi ou quoi ?

Jacques – What day is it today ?
Pierre – Listen ! I never know when I'm on holiday.
Jacques – There must be somone who can tell us.
Pierre – Look at that lady's newspaper : Wednesday, August 15th.
The lady – No, young man. It's the newspaper from the day before yesterday.
Jacques – Thank you. So, it's Friday, August 17th.
Pierre – What year ?
Jacques – That's a bit much ! Are you pulling my leg ?

Dates 12

Dates in French are presented as follows: the day of the week, followed by the date, the month and the year: jeudi, 1er août 1992.

In principle, the first letter of the day and the month should be spelt with a small letter but many French people use capitals. When giving the date orally it isn't necessary to specify the day: "Nous sommes le 1er août 1992". Note that French differs from English in using cardinal numbers, and not ordinals, for dates. The only exception is the first of the month: "le premier août", followed by "le deux août" (2 août), "le trois août" (3 août) ... "le vingt et un août" (21 août), etc. The important dates in a person's life are his/her "anniversaire" (birthday), "anniversaire de mariage" (wedding anniversary) and feast day ("fête") when his/her name is the same as the saint's name in the Catholic calendar.

VOCABULARY

lundi	Monday
mardi	Tuesday
mercredi	Wednesday
jeudi	Thursday
vendredi	Friday
samedi	Saturday
dimanche	Sunday
janvier	January
février	February
mars	March
avril	April
mai	May
juin	June
juillet	July
août	August
septembre	September
octobre	October
novembre	November
décembre	December
un agenda	diary
aujourd'hui	today
demain	tomorrow
hier	yesterday
un calendrier	calendar

GRAMMAR

Impersonal constructions :

- Indefinite pronouns make it possible to avoid specifying the subject of the sentence.
– for people and animals : **personne ... ne** (nobody), **quelqu'un** (somebody), **n'importe qui** (anybody)
– for objects : **tout** (everything), **quelque chose** (something), **n'importe quoi** (anything), **rien ... ne** (nothing)
- The construction « **il** » + certain so-called « impersonal » verbs is used when talking about natural phenomena.
Il pleut. Il neige. Il fait beau/mauvais/soleil.

▲ These verbs only exist in the third person singular.

- Expressing necessity : « **il faut** » + infinitive
Il faut réfléchir avant de parler.

EXERCISES

1. Complete the sentences with :

il faut – quelqu'un – il pleut – personne
Comme ..... je prends mon parapluie.
Non, vraiment, je ne sais pas, ... ne peut vous renseigner.
..... vous demande, Monsieur le directeur.
Pour traverser une rue, ... faire attention.

2. Find the questions that gave the following answers. Use an indefinite pronoun.

Non, je n'ai besoin de rien. → Tu as besoin de quelque chose ?
Non, je n'ai rencontré personne.
Non, je ne veux rien.
Non, je ne connais personne.

3. Complete the following sentences with « il faut ».

Pour aller vite de Paris à New York, ... (avion). Elle est malade, ... (médecin). Pour mieux voir, ... (lunettes).

KEY TO EXERCISES

1. il pleut – personne – Quelqu'un – il faut.
2. Vous avez rencontré quelqu'un ? Tu veux quelque chose ? Tu connais quelqu'un ?
3. il faut prendre l'avion. il faut appeler un médecin. il faut des lunettes.

HOW TO SAY IT !

Exprimer son ignorance, son incertitude, un doute :

– Ça, je ne sais pas.
– Je n'en sais rien.
– Qui sait ?
– Ça alors...
– Je me demande si...
– Je suis désolée, je ne me souviens vraiment pas.

Expressing one's ignorance, uncertainty, doubt :

– I don't know (about that).
– I have no idea.
– Who knows ?
– Well I never ...
– I wonder if ...
– I'm sorry. I really don't remember.

Today is D-day.

Douane

– Bonjour, monsieur. Votre passeport, s'il vous plaît.
– Voilà.
– Vous êtes mexicain ?
– Oui.
– Pourquoi venez-vous en France ?
– Je viens pour étudier, j'ai une bourse.
– Vous allez loger où ?
– Chez des amis, à Grenoble.
– Votre visa est en règle. Vous n'avez rien à déclarer ?
– Non, rien de particulier.
– Ouvrez votre valise, s'il vous plaît... Voyons... c'est quoi ça ?
– Un flacon de parfum.
– Ça va. Allez-y et bon séjour en France !

– Good morning/afternoon, sir. Your passport, please.
– Here you are.
– You're Mexican ?
– Yes
– Why are you coming to France ?
– I'm coming to study. I've got a grant.
– Where are you going to stay ?
– With friends, in Grenoble.
– Your visa's in order. Have you nothing to declare ?
– No, nothing in particular.
– Open your case, please... Well, now... What's this ?
– A bottle of perfume.
– Okay. On you go, and have a pleasant stay in France !

BON À SAVOIR

French Customs and Excise is present not only at the frontiers, airports and ports (maritime and inland) but also throughout the French territory (at least one office in each department, plus mobile teams, known as "la douane volante" or the flying customs).
Its role is to uphold the law and to fight those who break it (drugs and other trafficking).
To enter France, tourists must present a passport or identity card.
A visa is required for certain foreign nationals.
Foreigners living in France must posses a residence permit: the "carte de séjour".
No special vaccinations are required.

VOCABULARY

l'âge	age	**le tourisme**	tourism
célibataire	single	**l'alcool**	alcohol
divorcé(e)	divorced	**l'argent**	money
marié(e)	married	**des cigarettes**	cigarettes
la nationalité	nationality	**une valise**	suitcase
le nom	name	**les bagages**	baggage
le prénom	first name	**un passeport**	passport
le sexe	sex	**un visa**	visa
veuf(ve)	widower (widow)	**contrôler**	to inspect
les affaires	belongings	**déclarer**	to declare
les études	studies	**fouiller**	to search,
la profession	profession	**remplir**	to fill out

GRAMMAR

▮ *Negation :*

- of a sentence : « **non** » **:** *Vous habitez en France ?* → *Non, j'habite au Mexique.*
- of a verb :

– **Ne** + verb + **pas/rien/personne/aucun :**
Je ne suis pas français.
– **Ne** + auxiliary + **pas** + past participle :
Je n'ai pas eu de chance.

▲ When the articles « **un, une, des** » are preceded by a negation, they become « **de/des** » **:**
Il a un passeport ? → Non, il n'a pas **de** *passeport.*

- of a infinitive : « **ne pas** » + infinitive :
Ne pas *fumer.*

EXERCISES

1. Reply in the negative to the following questions.

Tu as eu des problèmes à la douane ? → Non, je n'ai pas eu de problèmes à la douane.

Vous avez quelque chose à déclarer ? Il connaît quelqu'un en France ? Elle a ses bagages ? Vous avez vos papiers ?

2. Find the appropriate negation for each situation.

a) Dans un train	1. Ne pas se présenter sans visa.
b) Dans un lieu public	2. Ne pas se pencher au-dehors.
c) À la gare	3. Ne pas fumer.
d) À la douane	4. Ne pas arriver en retard.

3. Translate.

Les douaniers m'ont fouillé. J'ai déclaré que j'avais deux bouteilles d'alcool. Il n'a pas besoin de visa pour entrer en France.

KEY TO EXERCISES

1. Je n'ai rien à déclarer. Il ne connaît personne en France. Elle n'a pas ses bagages. Je n'ai pas mes papiers.
2. a. 2 – b. 3 – c. 4 – d. 1.
3. The customs officers searched me. I declared that I had two bottles of spirits. He doesn't need a visa to enter France.

HOW TO SAY IT !

Le douanier s'adresse au voyageur :

– D'où venez-vous ?
– Où allez-vous ?
– Vous avez quelque chose à déclarer ?
– Vous restez combien de temps ?
– Ouvrez votre sac / valise, s'il vous plaît !
– Veuillez remplir et signer ce document !

A customs officer speaking to a traveller :

– Where are you (coming) from ?
– Where are you going ?
– Do you have anything to declare ?
– How long are you staying ?
– Open your bag/suitcase, please !
– Would you fill in and sign this document !

I would like political asylum !
(asile = place of refuge)

Marseille, le 2 mars

Madame le proviseur,

J'ai bien reçu votre lettre dans laquelle vous vous plaignez du comportement de mon fils Jacques.

Il semble qu'il ait été insolent envers son professeur d'anglais, à la suite de quoi il a été renvoyé du cours pour la semaine. À son retour, Jacques n'avait apporté ni son livre ni son cahier.

Le professeur a décidé de le faire passer en conseil de discipline. Cette mesure me paraît bien excessive à la veille du baccalauréat. C'est pourquoi je sollicite de votre bienveillance d'examiner à nouveau son cas.

Recevez, Madame le proviseur, mes salutations les meilleures.

Madeleine Rioux

Marseille, March 2nd

Dear Mrs ....,

I acknowledge receipt of your letter in which you complain about the behaviour of my son, Jacques.

It appears that he was rude to his English teacher, following which he was barred from the class for a week. When he returned, Jacques had neither his textbook nor his exercise book with him.

The teacher decided to send him before the disciplinary committee. This measure seems to me to be very excessive on the eve of the baccalauréat. This is why I ask if you would be good enough to reconsider his case.

Thanking you in advance, Yours faithfully,

Madeleine Rioux

BON À SAVOIR

State education is "gratuite, laïque et obligatoire" (free, non-religious and compulsory) from the ages of 6 to 16. State schools are run by the "Ministère de l'Education Nationale" (Ministry of Education).

Education is divided into a number of "cycles":

- "la maternelle" (nursery school) (from 3 to 6 - not compulsory);

- "le primaire" (primary school) (lasting 5 years);

- "le secondaire" (secondary school) "le collège" (lasting 4 years) then "le lycée" (lasting 3 years);

- "le supérieur" (higher education): university ("la faculté") or "les grandes écoles" (high-level technical institutions sometimes equated with Oxbridge).

In the first three cycles, lessons are held in the mornings and afternoons (except on Wednesdays and Saturday afternoons).

A number of diplomas are awarded at the end of secondary school: the "certificat d'aptitude professionnel" (C.A.P.) or the "brevet d'enseignement professionnel (B.E.P.) after the "collège" and the "baccalauréat" (or "le bac" - equivalent to "A" levels in England) after the lycée.

VOCABULARY

un directeur	headmaster
un enseignant	teacher
un(e) instituteur(trice)	(primary school) teacher
un principal	principal
un professeur (prof)	teacher
le lycée	secondary school
la maternelle	nursery school
le primaire	primary school
le secondaire	secondary school
le supérieur	higher education
l'université	university
une classe	class
un cours	lesson, course
une discipline	discipline
l'éducation	education
l'enseignement	education, teaching
le baccalauréat	(equivalent GCE "A" levels)
un examen	exam
un horaire	timetable
les matières	subjects
une option	option
la récréation	break, playtime
une salle	classroom
une section	section

GRAMMAR

■ *The negation «ni» :*

ne... ni... ni – ni... ni... ne

*Je **n'**ai **ni** amis **ni** ennemis.*
***Ni** lui **ni** elle **n'**aiment le fromage.*

■ *The relative preceded by a preposition and an adverbial phrase of place :*

de, par, à, dans, en → où, d'où, par où, dans lequel, etc. :

*Le lycée **d'où** je viens.*

EXERCISES

1. Transform the following sentences into the negative form.

Il sait lire et écrire. → Il ne sait ni lire ni écrire.

J'ai choisi le latin et le grec.
Dans ce village il y a un collège et un lycée.
Nous aimons les mathématiques et les lettres.

2. Match the following to make complete sentences.

1. L'école	a) dans lequel il y a ce poème est épuisé.
2. L'université	b) où vont les jeunes enfants a 5 classes.
3. Le collège	c) par laquelle il est passé est réputée.
4. Le livre	d) d'où je viens prépare bien au lycée.

3. Translate.

C'est au lycée que les élèves choisissent leurs options.
Ils ont cours de langue au moins trois fois par semaine.
Il faut le baccalauréat pour s'inscrire à l'université.
Ma mère est professeur dans ce lycée.

KEY TO EXERCISES

1. Je n'ai choisi ni le latin ni le grec. Dans ce village il n'y a ni collège ni lycée. Nous n'aimons ni les mathématiques ni les lettres.
2. 1.b – 2.c – 3.d – 4.a.
3. It's in secondary school that pupils choose their options. They have a language class at least three times a week. You need the baccalauréat to get into university. My mother is a teacher in this secondary school.

HOW TO SAY IT !

POUR ÉCRIRE UNE LETTRE OFFICIELLE.

• Pour commencer :

Mademoiselle, Madame, Monsieur. Cher/chère (si l'on connaît la personne).

• Pour finir :

Croyez, (chère) Mademoiselle, (chère) Madame, (cher) Monsieur, en l'assurance de mes sentiments les meilleurs (si l'on connaît la personne).
Je vous prie d'agréer, Mademoiselle, Madame, Monsieur, mes sincères salutations.

WRITING AN OFFICIAL LETTER.

• How to start :

Miss, Madam, Sir, Dear ... (if you know your correspondent)

• How to conclude :

All formal endings equivalent to « Yours sincerely/faithfully ». Only use « cher / chère » if you knows your correspondent personally.

My friend's an egghead !

Jean-Pierre : John, je te présente ma famille. Mon père.

Le père : Bonjour.

John : Bonjour, monsieur.

Jean-Pierre : Ma mère.

La mère : Enchantée.

John : Bonjour, madame.

Jean-Pierre : Mon grand-père et ma grand-mère qui passent quelques jours à Paris mais ils habitent à Rouen.

Les grands-parents : Monsieur !

John : Ah ! Ravi de vous connaître.

Jean-Pierre : Eh bien voilà, tu connais tout le monde. Ah ! non, lui, c'est Grison, notre chat.

Le père : Bien, les présentations sont faites. On peut passer à table.

Jean-Pierre : John, I'd like you to meet my family. My father.
The father : How d'you do.
John : How d'you do.
Jean-Pierre : My mother.
The mother : Delighted.
John : How d'you do.
Jean-Pierre : My grandfather and my grandmother, who are spending a few days in Paris but live in Rouen.

The grand parents : 'Evening !
John : Very pleased to meet you.
Jean-Pierre : Well, there you are. Now you know everyone. Oh ! No (I forgot), this is Grison, our cat.
The father : Well, now we've been introduced, we can all sit down and eat.

Until recently, French life was largely based upon the family. Nowadays, the family unit is smaller and organised differently. People move house more often for professional reasons, both husband and wife go out to work, they have fewer children (fewer than 3 on average) and the divorce rate has increased a great deal (almost 1 in 4 marriages end in divorce). But the family remains extremely important to most French people – they get together whenever they can, on Sundays or during the holidays.

Some statistics: 90% of 18-year olds live with their parents in France, 50% of 22-year olds and 25% of 24-year olds, and 25% of children under the age of 18 have experimented with drugs!

1 out of 5 French people are aged 65 or more – this will rise to 1 out of 4 by the year 2010.

VOCABULARY

le concubinage	cohabitation	**une fille**	daughter
un divorce	divorce	**les grands-parents**	grandparents
un mariage	marriage, wedding	**les petits-enfants**	grandchildren
une naissance	birth	**les beaux-parents**	in-laws
un bébé	baby	**le beau-père**	father-in-law
les parents	parents	**la belle-mère**	mother-in-law
un père (papa)	father (dad)	**la belle-fille (la bru)**	daughter-in-law
une mère (maman)	mother (mum)	**le gendre**	son-in-law
un mari	husband	**un cousin**	cousin
une femme	wife	**un neveu**	nephew
les enfants	children	**un oncle**	uncle
un fils	son	**une tante**	aunt

GRAMMAR

Conjunctions :

• Coordinating conjunctions link words or groups of words together : **or** (now, in fact) ; **mais** (but) ; **ou** (or) ; **et** (and) ; **donc** (therefore) ; **ni** (neither) ; **car** (for, because).

Je pense donc je suis.

• Subordinating conjunctions link a subordinate clause to another clause : **dès que** (as soon as) ; **quand** (when) ; **que** (which, that) ; **lorsque** (when) ; **pendant que** (while)

Il a plu pendant une semaine.

EXERCISES

1. Choose* «donc» *or* «car» *to make single sentences, as in the example.

Il pleut. Je prends mon parapluie. → Il pleut, donc je prends mon parapluie.

Elle se dépêche. Elle est en retard.
Tu la connais. Je te l'ai présentée.
Il n'est pas là demain. Je n'irai pas chez lui.
Il est malade. Il ne sortira pas.

***2. Complete with* «lorsque - dès que - que - quand».**

Vous pouvez venir ..... vous voudrez.
..... nous sommes arrivés chez nos parents, il a plu.
Nous les recevrons ..... les travaux seront terminés.
J'aimerais ..... tu regardes mon album de photos.

3. Give the appropriate conjunction.

Deux ..... deux font quatre.
La boulangerie reste ouverte ..... les travaux.
Je ferai des études de français .... d'anglais.
Allez-y ..... ne rentrez pas trop tard.
Ils ont rendu visite à leur grand-mère ..... elle est malade.

KEY TO EXERCISES

1. car - car - donc - donc.
2. quand - dès que / lorsque - lorsque / dès que - que.
3. et - pendant - ou - mais - car.

HOW TO SAY IT !

ACCUEILLIR/RECEVOIR QUELQU'UN :

- **Bienvenu(e) !**
- **Fais comme chez toi.**
- **Vous êtes ici chez vous.**
- **Asseyez-vous, je vous en prie.**
- **Mettez-vous à l'aise.**
- **Tu bois quelque chose ?**
- **Je peux vous offrir quelque chose ?**

GREETING/WELCOMING SOMEONE :

- *Welcome !*
- *Make yourself at home.*
- *Consider yourself at home.*
- *Please sit down.*
- *Make yourself comfortable.*
- *Would you like something to drink ?*
- *Can I offer you something ?*

Let's not wash our dirty linen in public !

Danèze/Rapho

Azay-le-Rideau.

Mini-guide : the Provinces

France is the second most popular country in the world for tourism. It attracts most visitors in July and August (the warmest months of the year).

Famous sites and monuments

France is exceptionally rich in places of interest and visitors are constantly faced with an agonizing *"embarras du choix"* when trying to decide what to see. Depending upon how much time you have at your disposal, we recommend the following :

• **Sites**
Saint Michael's Mount ("Le Mont Saint-Michel") between Brittany and Normandy.
The Normandy beaches (scene of the D-day landings during the Second World War).
The prehistoric remains at Carnac, Brittany.
The sea of ice at Chamonix, near the Mont-Blanc (in the Alps).
The Gorges of the Tarn ("Gorges du Tarn").
The bays of Corsica (notably "le Golfe de Porto").

• **Monuments**
The Roman Theatre in Orange.
The "Palais des Papes" (Popes' Palace) in Avignon.
The Châteaux of the Loire (Chambord, Blois, Chenonceaux...) and other castles in Angers, Pau, Carcassonne...
Medieval cathedrals : Albi, Bourges, Chartres, Poitiers, Reims, Rouen, Strasbourg, Toulouse...
Romanesque churches in the Auvergne.
Monastries and abbeys all over France...

• **Museums**
The Toulouse-Lautrec museum in Albi, southern France.
The museums in Caen and Bayeux (with its famous tapestry) in the north-west and the museums in Nancy, Strasbourg, Colmar in the east.

... as well as the Chagall museum in Nice, the "musée de la Préhistoire aux Eyzies" in the Dordogne, the museum in Pau...

– Bonjour, Paul. C'est Raoul.
– Ah ! Raoul. Ça fait une éternité ! Ça va ?
– Oui, pas mal. Justement, j'aimerais bien te voir. Tu es libre en fin de semaine ?
– Non, je fais le pont du 1er mai : je pars dès mercredi.
– Ah ! bon. Et la semaine d'après ?
– Il y a le 8 mai.
– Oui et après viennent l'Ascension et la Pentecôte ! On ne se verra jamais !
– Mais si, on y arrivera... mais pas avant la fin du mois !

– Hello Paul. It's Raoul.
– Ah, Raoul. Haven't heard from you for ages. How are things ?
– Fine. In fact, I'd like to see you. Are you free at the end of the week ?
– No, I'm taking a long weekend for the 1st of May : I'm leaving on Wednesday.
– Oh really. And the week after ?
– There's the 8th of May.
– Yes, and after that come the Ascension and Whitsun ! We'll never see each other !
– Yes, we'll manage... but not before the end of the month.

Bank holidays 16

BON À SAVOIR

In addition to the usual religious (Catholic) festivals – Easter ("Paques"), Ascension ("Ascension"), Whitsun ("Pentecôte") – there are several secular bank holidays in France: 1st January: New Year's Day. 1st May: Labour Day. 8th May: Victory of 1945. 14th July: national holiday (the storming of the Bastille, 1789). 11th November: Armistice of 1918. If you are visiting France on the 11th November or the 8th May, you will see commemorative celebrations wherever you happen to be: public figures placing flowers on cenotaphs, troops parading in the streets... But it is in Paris, on the 14th July, that the ceremonies are the most spectacular. Thousands of soldiers march down the Champs-Elysées while planes and helicopters fly overhead.

Public services (banks, post offices, government offices) are closed on bank holidays. Some shops, theatres and cinemas, however, usually remain open.

VOCABULARY

un anniversaire	birthday
un calendrier	calendar
un congé	holiday
un jour férié	bank holiday
fin de semaine	week-end
le repos	rest
le travail	work
les vacances	holidays
un «pont»	long holiday week-end
une fanfare	fanfare
un feu d'artifice	fireworks
la grasse matinée	a long lie in bed
un hommage	tribute, respects
une kermesse	fair, charity fête
un monument aux morts	cenotaph
une visite	visit
des vœux	(best) wishes
civil(e)	civil
national(e)	national
religieux(euse)	religious
célébrer	to celebrate
commémorer	to commemorate
défiler	to march, parade
travailler	to work

GRAMMAR

▮ *The verb* «être» :

«**Être**» is both a verb and an auxiliary. It is used in the conjugation of a certain number of verbs in the compound tenses.

Present : je suis, tu es, nous sommes...
Imperfect : j'étais, tu étais, nous étions...
Future : je serai, tu seras, nous serons...
Perfect : j'ai été, tu as été, nous avons été...
Conditional : je serais, tu serais, nous serions...
Pluperfect : j'avais été, tu avais été, nous avions été...
Past Conditional : j'aurais été ... nous aurions été...
Present subjunctive : que je sois ... que nous soyons...
Imperative : sois, soyons, soyez.

EXERCISES

***1. Complete using the present indicative of the verb* «être».**

Mon frère et moi ..... argentins. .....-vous en congé ? C'est moi qui ..... en retard ! .....-elle toujours en vacances ? C'est toujours toi qui ..... le dernier.

2. Conjugate the verb* «être» *in the tenses given in brackets.

Il faut que vous (present subjunctive) ponctuels. Tu (perfect) malade ? (imperative) patient et tu (future) récompensé. Si tu (imperfect) raisonnable tu fumerais moins. Quand je (future) vieux, je lirai beaucoup.

3. Answer the questions as in the example.

Vous êtes brésiliens, messieurs ? → Oui, nous sommes brésiliens.

Tu es marié, Paul ? On est en avance ? Nous sommes en retard ? Je suis en avance.

KEY TO EXERCISES

1. sommes – êtes – suis – est – es.
2. soyez – as été – Sois / seras - étais – serai.
3. Oui, je suis marié. Oui, vous êtes en avance. Oui, vous êtes en retard. Oui, tu es en avance.

HOW TO SAY IT !

PRÉSENTER SES VŒUX :	**PRESENTING ONE'S BEST WISHES :**
– Je vous souhaite une bonne année.	*– Happy New Year !*
– Je te souhaite une bonne santé.	*– Good health !*
– Je vous souhaite tout ce que vous désirez.	*– May you have everything you want !*
– Acceptez mes vœux pour ce nouvel an.	*– All the best for the new year !*
– Je vous présente mes vœux pour la nouvelle année.	*– My best wishes for the new year !*
– Bonne année !	*– Happy New Year !*
– Joyeux Noël !	*– Merry Christmas !*
– Passez de bonnes fêtes (de fin d'année) !	*– Enjoy yourself at Christmas and the New Year !*

We're having a ball !
(s'éclater = to explode / have a great time)

Du nord au sud et d'est en ouest, chaque région de France est jalouse de ses richesses, de ses particularités et de ses vins.

Allez dans le Nord, vous y mangerez la flamiche (tarte aux poireaux) et le lapin aux pruneaux arrosés de bière ou de vin rouge. Dans l'Est, la choucroute est excellente : mangez-en en buvant une bonne bière ou un vin blanc d'Alsace. Les côtes de la Manche ou de l'Atlantique vous offrent poissons et fruits de mer. Dans le Centre, chaque région a ses spécialités culinaires.

Connaissez-vous la bouillabaisse ? Non ! Alors une halte s'impose au vieux port de Marseille pour déguster cette délicieuse soupe de poissons !

(Le guide du bien-manger)

From north to south and from east to west, each region of France is jealous of its riches, its distinctive produce and wines.

Go to the north and you will eat flamiche (leek pie) and rabbit with prunes cooked in beer or red wine. In the east, the sauerkraut is excellent : eat it with a good beer or a white wine from Alsace. The Channel and Atlantic coasts offer fish and seafood. In the Centre, each region has its culinary specialties.

Do you know bouillabaisse ? No ! Well then, you must stop at the old port of Marseilles to taste this delicious fish soup !

BON À SAVOIR

Eating habits have changed since the seventies, especially for the midday meal. Instead of the "traditional" lunch, now considered heavy and excessively rich in calories, the French now tend to eat a variety of salads, grilled meat accompanied by green vegetables ...

For the evening meal, restaurateurs propose "la nouvelle cuisine" - a new kind of lighter dishes where greater importance is attached to the way the food is presented on the plate.

Gourmets should make sure they taste some fresh foie gras (from the Landes region), accompanied by a good Sauternes for example. Or, if you prefer meat, a "magret de canard" (duck cutlet), a "poularde de Bresse" (fatted chicken from Bresse) or "une pièce de Charolais" (a Charolais steak). French cheese, of course, is world famous, boasting more than 300 different varieties!

VOCABULARY

un dessert	dessert
du fromage	cheese
de la soupe	soup
un (du) vin (blanc, rouge, rosé)	wine (white, red, rosé)
le goût	taste
un guide	guide
un plat	dish
des produits (alimentaires)	foodstuffs, produce
une recette	recipe
une spécialité	speciality
régional(e)	regional
le terroir	soil, rural origin
un chef (de cuisine)	chef
un(e) cuisinier(ière)	cook
un garçon	waiter
une serveuse	waitress
un gourmand	gourmand
un gourmet	gourmet, epicure
un gastronome	gastronome
savoureux(euse)	tasty
apprécier	to appreciate
choisir	to choose
déguster	to taste, savour
goûter	to taste

GRAMMAR

▮ *The pronouns «en» and «y» :*

En and **y** replace nouns or pronouns.

- **En** can mean **de cela :** *Prends du vin ! Prends-**en** !*
- **En** can mean **de là** (place) : *Vous venez de Paris ? J'**en** viens.*
- **Y** can mean **là :** *Tu vas à Paris ? J'**y** vais.*
- **Y** can also mean **à cela** (à lui, à elle...) :

  *Tu penses à tes vacances ? J'**y** pense.*

▲ With the future and conditional tenses of the verb «**aller**», «**y**» disappears : *Tu iras à Rome ? Oui, j'irai.*

EXERCISES

1. Answer the following questions using «en».

Tu manges souvent du foie gras ? → Non, j'en mange seulement à Noël.

Ils achètent des gâteaux tous les jours ? Oui... Elle prend du sucre dans son café ? Non... Tu viens de ton travail ? Oui... Vous reprenez du fromage ? Oui...

2. Answer the following questions using «y».

Le vin blanc est au frais ? → Oui, il y est.

Vous travaillez dans ce magasin ? Vous mangez souvent au restaurant ? Tu penses à la réception ? Tu vas chercher le pain ?

3. Complete using «en» or «y».

Vous aimez ce gâteau ? Reprenez- ..... .
Alors on ..... va ? Il connaît bien les vins, il ..... parle tout le temps. Qu'est-ce que c'est ? Une spécialité ? Oh ! J' ..... veux. Cette sauce est terminée : nous ..... avons mis le temps !

KEY TO EXERCISES

1. Oui, ils en achètent tous les jours. Non, elle n'en prend pas. Oui, j'en viens. Oui, j'en reprends.
2. Oui, j'y travaille (nous y travaillons) depuis cinq ans. Oh ! oui, nous y mangeons souvent. Mais oui, j'y pense.Oui, j'y vais.
3. en – y – en – en – y.

HOW TO SAY IT !

POUR COMMANDER :

– Comme entrée / pour commencer, des poireaux.
– Ensuite / comme plat, je prendrais une entrecôte.
– Pour terminer / comme dessert, un sorbet citron.
– Mettez-nous un beaujolais avec le fromage.

ORDERING A MEAL :

– Leeks to begin with, as a starters.
– Then, for the main course, I'll take an entrecôte steak.
– A lemon sorbet to finish /for dessert.
– Give us a beaujolais with the cheese.

DEMANDER UN CONSEIL AU MAÎTRE D'HÔTEL :

– Quelle est votre spécialité ?
– Quel est le plat du jour ?
– Quelle(s) est(sont) la(les) suggestion(s) du chef ?
– Quel vin me(nous) conseillez-vous avec ce plat ?

ASKING THE HEAD WAITER FOR ADVICE :

– What is your speciality ?
– What's the dish of the day ?
– What is/are the chef's suggestion(s) ?
– What wine do you recommend with this dish ?

I could eat a horse !
(crocs = fangs)

– Tu penses quoi de ce manteau ?
– Il n'est pas mal, mais je trouve que celui que tu viens d'essayer est plus chic, la couleur est superbe et il est mieux coupé.
– Mais il est beaucoup plus cher. Il ne vaut pas mieux que j'achète celui-ci ? Il me semble plus pratique. Plus confortable aussi. Tu ne crois pas ?
– Oui, c'est vrai, mais si tu veux mon avis, l'autre fait plus d'effet et il te va mieux. C'est l'argument décisif, ça, non ?
– Tout à fait !

– What do you think of this coat ?
– It isn't bad, but I think the one you just tried on is smarter. The colour is superb and the cut is better.
– But it's much more expensive. Wouldn't it be better if I bought this one ? It seems more practical to me. More comfortable too. Don't you think so ?
– Yes, it's true but, if you want my opinion, the other one is more impressive and suits you better. That's the clinching argument, isn't it ?
– Absolutely !

Clothes

BON À SAVOIR

The French spend a lot of money on clothes - usually "prêt à porter" (off-the-peg) despite Paris' reputation as the fashion capital of the world!

The main "couturiers" (fashion designers) are world-famous (Courrèges, Dior, Yves Saint-Laurent, Chanel, Ted Lapidus ...) and a large part of their production is sold overseas.

The mail-order business ("vente par correspondance") has grown considerably in recent years. People choose what they want from a catalogue and order by mail or Minitel (paying directly with their banker's card). The most well-known companies are La Redoute and Les Trois Suisses.

VOCABULARY

une ceinture	belt
des chaussures	shoes
des gants	gloves
un costume	suit
une veste	jacket
une chemise	shirt
une cravate	tie
un manteau	coat
un imperméable	raincoat
un ensemble	ensemble, outfit
une robe	dress
un tailleur	suit (for women)
les sous-vêtements	underclothes
des bas	stockings
des collants	tights
la lingerie	lingerie, underwear
un slip	underpants, panties
un soutien-gorge	bra
un maillot (de bain)	swimming costume
un pyjama	pyjamas
(se) déshabiller	to get undressed
enlever	to take off
(s')habiller	to get dressed
porter	to wear

GRAMMAR

Irregular comparatives :

– adjective : bon/bonne → meilleur(e)
C'est un meilleur prix.
– adverb : bien → mieux
Cette veste te va mieux.
– adjective : mauvais(e) → pire
– adverb : mal → pire
La qualité est pire qu'on ne le pensait.

The subjunctive :

The subjunctive is used after certain expressions of judgement such as : « il vaut mieux que » (it's better that), « je ne pense pas que » (I don't think that), « il faut que » (it's necessary that), « je ne crois pas que » (I don't believe that).
La qualité est pire qu'on ne le pense. (penser)

EXERCISES

1. Transform using a comparative as in the example.

C'est encore mauvais ! → C'est encore pire !
Ces chaussures sont bonnes. Je trouve ça mauvais. Cette veste-là est bien.

2. Complete using a present subjunctive.

C'est le vêtement le plus élégant qui *(être).*
Il ne vaut mieux pas que tu *(venir)* au défilé de mode.
Il faut qu'on *(aller)* dans les magasins.

3. Translate.

Je crois que tu as tort d'acheter ce costume. Je ne pense pas que vous ayez raison de vous habiller comme ça. La jupe est plus élégante que la robe.

KEY TO EXERCISES

1. meilleures - pire - mieux.
2. soit - viennes - aille.
3. I think that you are wrong to buy this suit. I don't think that you are right to dress like that. The skirt is more elegant than the dress.

HOW TO SAY IT !

DONNER DES CONSEILS VESTIMENTAIRES :

– Ce soir, fais un effort, habille-toi !
– Retirez votre manteau.
– La tenue de soirée est de rigueur.
– Cette cravate va très bien avec ta chemise.
– Mets ta robe bleue.
– Ces deux couleurs ne vont pas ensemble.

GIVING ADVICE ABOUT CLOTHES :

– Make an effort this evening, get dressed !
– Take off your coat.
– Evening dress is compulsory.
– This tie goes very well with your shirt.
– Wear your blue skirt.
– Those two colours don't match.

He's dressed up to the nines.
(tirer = to draw, pull ; épingle = pin)

« Programme de la sixième journée de notre voyage. Demain, lever à 7 heures. Petit déjeuner servi à partir de 8 h 30 jusqu'à 9 heures. La visite du musée doit s'effectuer tôt dans la matinée, afin de pouvoir rejoindre le car à midi et demi.

Après la pause du déjeuner, l'après-midi sera libre pour ceux qui désirent faire quelques achats.

Mais attention ! rendez-vous au théâtre, au plus tard, à 9 heures moins le quart. Le spectacle est à 21 heures. Retour prévu à l'hôtel vers minuit. Rassurez-vous, vous pourrez vous reposer le lendemain. »

«Schedule for the sixth day of our trip. Tomorrow, rise at 7 o'clock. Breakfast served from 8.30 to 9. The visit to the museum must be made early in the morning so that we can return to the coach at half past twelve.

After the lunch-break, the afternoon will be free for those who want to do some shopping.

But remember, be at the theatre at a quarter to nine at the latest. The show is at 9 o'clock.

Return to the hotel around midnight. Don't worry, you can rest the next day.»

BON À SAVOIR

The French frequently use the 24-hour clock when speaking or writing about the time :
- in the morning, they say : "Il est 9 heures" (It's nine o'clock) ;
- at midday : "Il est midi" (It's midday), "Rendez-vous à 12 heures" (Appointment at 12 o'clock) ;
- in the afternoon : "Il est 4 heures et quart" or alternatively "Il est 16 heures 15" (It's a quarter past four) ;
- in the evening : "On se voit à 8 heures et demi" (We'll meet at half past eight) or "La séance est à 20 heures 30" (The performance is at 20. 30) ;
- at night : "Nous sommes rentré(e)s à minuit" (We got back at midnight) or "Le train est arrivé à 0h 52" (The train arrived at 0. 52).

France has standard summer time (two hours ahead of solar time) and standard winter time (one hour ahead). The clocks are changed at the beginning of spring and autumn.

VOCABULARY

une seconde	second	**un réveil**	alarm clock
une minute	minute	**la nuit**	night
une demi-heure	half-hour	**le soir**	evening
le jour	day	**la soirée**	evening (party)
le matin	morning	**le temps**	time, weather
la matinée	morning	**tard**	late
le souper	supper	**tôt**	early
une horloge	clock	**déjeuner**	to have lunch
nocturne	nocturnal	**dîner**	to have dinner
un moment	moment	**(se) lever**	to get up
un repas	meal	**(se) réveiller**	to wake up
la sieste	siesta, snooze	**(se) coucher**	to go to bed
une montre	watch	**s'écouler**	to pass (by)

GRAMMAR

▮ *Use of the verb in the infinitive :*

The infinitive is used :

- when it follows another verb (except « avoir » or « être ») :
  Tu peux venir.
- after a preposition or an interrogative pronoun :
  Pour partir...
  Avant de parler...
  Lequel choisir... ?
  Comment dire... ?
- it can be the subject :
  Dormir est nécessaire.

EXERCISES

1. Choose the appropriate word.

journée – minute – heures – heure

Le train part à neuf ..... . Attends une ..... j'arrive ! Il travaille toute la ..... ! À quelle ..... te lèves-tu ?

2. Transform the sentences as in the example (watch out for the agreements !).

J'ai lu la notice. → Je l'ai lue.

Il a passé la nuit dehors. Nous avons fait la sieste. On a attendu tes amies. Ils ont réveillé les enfants.

3. Translate.

Se lever tôt est pénible. J'ai besoin de café pour me réveiller. Tu dois te coucher tôt. Travaillez avant de déjeuner !

KEY TO EXERCISES

1. heures – minute – journée – heure.
2. Il l'a passée dehors. – Nous l'avons faite. – On les a attendues. – Ils les ont réveillés.
3. Getting up early is hard. I need coffee to wake me up. You must go to bed early. Work before having lunch.

HOW TO SAY IT !

COMMENT DEMANDER L'HEURE :

– Quelle heure est-il, s'il vous plaît ?
– Excusez-moi, il est quelle heure ?
– Pardon, vous avez l'heure ?

– Vous pourriez me donner l'heure ?

ASKING THE TIME :

– What time is it, please ?

– Excuse me, what time is it ?

– Excuse me, do you have the time ?
– Could you give me the time ?

COMMENT RENSEIGNER QUELQU'UN SUR UNE HEURE :

– Il est huit heures et demie !
– Le train part à dix heures moins le quart.
– Le magasin ouvre à quinze heures.
– Rendez-vous à la demie / au quart.

GIVING THE TIME :

– It's half past eight.
– The rain leaves at a quarter to ten.
– The shop opens at 3 o'clock p.m.
– Meeting time is at half past/a quarter past.

He goes to bed early.
(lit. : « He goes to bed with the hens »)

– Bonjour. Nous voudrions savoir s'il vous reste une chambre de libre... pour trois personnes : deux adultes et un enfant de cinq ans.

– Vous avez réservé ?

– Non.

– Un instant. Il nous reste une chambre pour deux personnes avec un grand lit, salle de bains, et vue sur la mer. Si vous voulez, nous pouvons rajouter un petit lit pour l'enfant.

– Oui, c'est très bien. Vous faites la demi-pension ?

– Bien sûr ! c'est 300 francs par personne et demi-tarif pour l'enfant. Le petit déjeuner est servi entre 7 h 30 et 10 h ; le dîner à partir de 19 heures.

– Parfait.

– Hello ! We'd like to know if you have a room available for three : two adults and a child of five.

– Have you reserved ?

– No.

– Just a minute. We have a room for two with a double bed, bathroom, and a sea view. If you like, we can add a small bed for the child.

– Yes, that's fine. Do you do half-board ?

– Of course ! And it's 300 francs per person and half-price for the child. Breakfast is served between 7.30 and 10 a.m. ; dinner from 7 p.m.

– Perfect.

Hotel-restaurant

To find a hotel, go to a tourist office or "syndicat d'initiative" where they can make a hotel reservation for you by telephone. Alternatively, a list of hotels is given in tourist guides, along with the categories to which they belong.

Checking-out time is midday in most hotels.

Hotels are classified as follows (the number of stars indicates the standard of comfort: bathroom or shower, environment, etc...):

****: very comfortable, ***: comfortable, **: reasonably comfortable, *: ordinary

Other types of accommodation are available: "gîtes ruraux" (self-catering country cottages), des "chambres chez l'habitant" (rooms in private houses), la "chambre et la table d'hôte" (rooms with board - often in the country), camping "à la ferme" (on farms), "Relais et Châteaux" (coaching inns and castles) ... the last two being rather expensive.

VOCABULARY

un maître d'hôtel	head waiter
un serveur	waiter, barman
une femme de ménage	cleaning lady
un ascenseur	lift
les bagages	baggage
une chambre	room
une clé	key
une douche	shower
les toilettes	toilet
une table	table
le menu	menu
la note	bill
une nuit	night
la pension (complète)	(full) board
le pourboire	tip
la réception	reception
un repas	meal
une réservation	reservation
le service (compris)	service charge (included)
un tarif	price list, rates
commander	to order
payer	to pay
régler	to settle
réserver	to reserve

GRAMMAR

▮ *Personal pronouns :*

The personal pronouns which follow a preposition are as follows :
singular : **moi, toi, lui/elle**
plural : **nous, vous, eux/elles**

*Il y a une réservation pour **nous**.*

▮ *The interrogative form :*

The interrogative can be expressed by inverting the subject and the verb (this style is found more in writing) :

On peut manger ? → Peut-on manger ?

EXERCISES

1. Choose the appropriate word.

ascenseur – régler – compris – bagages

Est-ce que je peux ..... avec une carte bancaire ?
Ici, le service est ..... .
Prenons l' ..... pour monter les ..... au 6e étage.

2. Use the appropriate personal pronoun as shown in the example.

Tu règles pour mes parents ? → Tu règles pour eux ?

Je pars avec mon fils.
Nous irons au restaurant avec Paul et Christine.
Tu as entendu parler de ce cuisinier ?
Il n'y avait personne avant ces clients.

3. Translate.

Je vais monter les bagages par l'ascenceur. Le pourboire est conseillé. Demande la clé à la réception.

KEY TO EXERCISES

1. régler – compris – ascenseur / bagages.
2. Je pars avec lui. Nous irons au restaurant avec eux. Tu as entendu parler de lui ? Il n'y avait personne avant eux.
3. I'll take the baggage up in the lift. Tipping is recommended. Ask for the key at the reception.

HOW TO SAY IT !

FAIRE UNE OFFRE, UNE PROPOSITION :

– Nous sommes complets, mais si vous voulez...
– Nous pourrions peut-être...
– Il est possible...
– On peut s'arranger...

MAKING AN OFFER, SUGGESTION :

– We're full, but if you like ...

– We could perhaps....
– It's possible....
– We can arrange to....

DONNER UN CONSEIL :

– Il faudrait que vous appeliez dès ce soir.
– Il vaudrait mieux appeler avant.
– Vous devriez réserver.
– À votre place, j'essaierais...

– Si j'étais toi...

RECOMMENDING OR ADVISING :

– You should call this evening.

– It would be better to call first.
– You should reserve.
– If I were you, I would try to....
– If I were you....

It looks as if the bill's going to be steep !
(salé = salted / expensive)

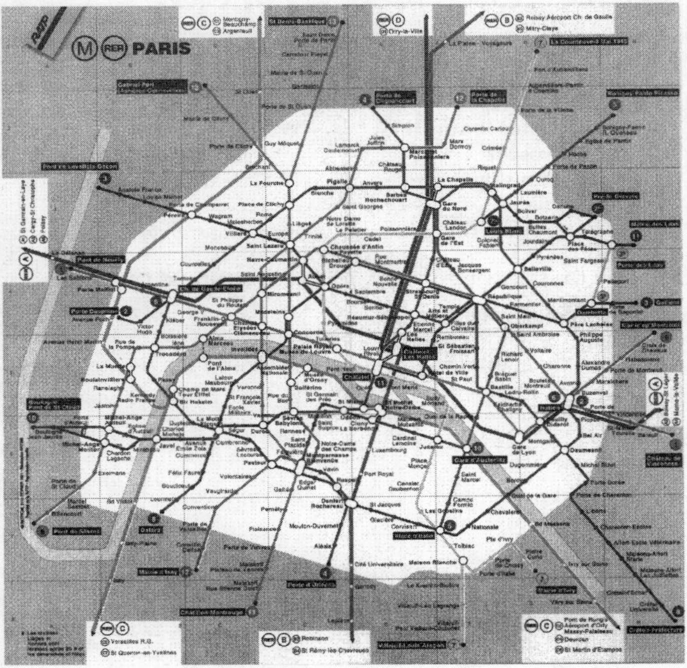

Info n° 4

Plan du métro parisien RATP 1991.

National museums

Museums are closed on Tuesdays, except the Musée Rodin and the Musée d'Orsay which are closed on Mondays. Entry is free for young people less than 18.

The following museums are all worth the visit :
• *le musée des Arts et Traditions populaires* (6, avenue du Mahatma-Gandhi, 16th arrondissement) • le *musée Picasso* (hôtel Salé, 5 rue de Thorigny, 3rd arr.) • le *musée Rodin* (hôtel Biron, 77, rue de Varenne, 7th arr.) • le *musée de l'Homme* (place de Trocadéro, 16th arr.) and, of course, the *Louvre,* the *musée d'Orsay* (1, rue de Bellechasse, 7th arr.), le *musée de Cluny* (6, place Paul-Painlevé, 5th arr.).
Be sure to visit the *Pompidou Centre* and the *Grand-Palais* (just off the Champs-Elysées).

Monuments and curiosities

In Paris : the Eiffel Tower *("tour Eiffel")* • *l'Arc de Triomphe* • La *Conciergerie* • les *Invalides* • *Notre-Dame* cathedral • Le *Sacré Cœur* ... but also the Montparnasse Tower • le Père Lachaise cemetry • a tour of the Paris sewers (13, quai d'Orsay, 7th arr.) or les Catacombes (1, place Denfert-Rochereau, 14th arr.) and lastly, the Garnier Opera House, the new Opéra-Bastille and the La Villette Centre for Science and Industry.
Also allow time to visit La Défense with its monumental *Arche.*

The Paris region

Don't miss :
• Versailles (the château - closed on Mondays -, the "Trianon", the "Hameau de la Reine" (the Queen's Hamlet), the palace grounds and the "grand canal"). Allow a full day!
In June and September, different events are organised including a water show with all the fountains turned on ("les grandes eaux").
• Fontainebleau (the château, grounds and museum) but also Chantilly, Compiègne, Saint-Germain (châteaux and museums).

N.B. : A special museum entry ticket ("carte inter-musées") is available from underground stations, museums and the Paris Office of Tourism. It gives entry to more than 60 museums and monuments, without having to queue!

Luis : J'ai un problème. Je suis invité par les parents d'un copain de fac, Jean-Pierre.

Marc : Eh bien, c'est parfait, tu vas connaître un peu la vie d'une famille française.

Luis : Oui, mais comment je dois m'habiller, moi ? Il faut que j'apporte quelque chose ?

Marc : Ça dépend. Tu connais ses parents ? Qu'est-ce qu'ils font ?

Luis : Ça, j'en sais rien. C'est important ?

Marc : Un peu. Tu es seul à être invité ?

Luis : Oui, je crois.

Marc : Si c'est un dîner en famille, pas de problème, habille-toi comme d'habitude, et c'est tout.

Luis : Et qu'est-ce que j'apporte ?

Marc : Oh ! Un beau bouquet de fleurs pour la maîtresse de maison.

Luis : I have a problem. I've been invited by the parents of a friend from university, Jean-Pierre.

Marc : Well, that's perfect. You'll get to know a little about life in a French family.

Luis : Yes, but what should I wear ? Must I bring (them) something ?

Marc : That depends. Do you know his parents ? What do they do ?

Luis : I have no idea. It is important ?

Marc : A little. Are you the only guest ?

Luis : Yes, I think so.

Marc : If it's an informal dinner, no problem, wear what you usually would. That's all.

Luis : And what do I take ?

Marc : Oh ! A nice bunch of flowers for the hostess.

If you receive an invitation from some French people, it will almost certainly be to share a meal (usually dinner in the evening, or Sunday lunch if the meal is informal).
It's always a good idea to bring something – flowers or a good bottle of wine. It's possible to bring a cake or a dessert but only when the meal is between friends and very informal.
A foreign visitor could bring a souvenir from his or her country.
Lunch is usually at 12.30 and dinner at 7.30 or 8 o'clock in the evening. It's considered bad form to arrive at the appointed hour precisely (or earlier!). Try to arrive 10 or 15 minutes late to give your hosts a few extra minutes to finalize their preparations.

VOCABULARY

un accueil	welcome
un apéritif	aperitif
un café	coffee
un cadeau	gift
un carton d'invitation	invitation card
un dîner	dinner
un goûter	tea (afternoon snack)
une invitation à **- déjeuner** **- danser**	invitation - to lunch - to dance
une réception	reception
une soirée	party
la vie sociale	social life
un hôte	host
une hôtesse	hostess
un(e) invité(e)	guest
la maîtresse de maison	hostess, housewife
bienvenu(e)	welcome
connaître	to know
faire l'honneur de...	to do (sb) the honnour of...
s'habiller	to get dressed
offrir	to offer
recevoir	to receive
sortir	to go out
rencontrer	to meet

GRAMMAR

Disjunctive pronouns :

Subject pronouns **(je, tu, il /elle, nous, vous, ils /elles)** can be emphasized by adding a disjunctive pronoun (also known as « emphatic pronouns ») : **moi, toi, lui /elle, nous, vous, eux /elles :** *Comment faut-il que je m'habille, moi ?*

«On», *indefinitive pronoun :*

«On» is used :

- to replace «**nous**» : *On vient à 18 h.*
- to replace **«tu»** or **«vous» :** *Alors on se promène ?* (ironic and condescending)
- with a collective meaning : « *On n'a rien sans rien.* » (proverb)

EXERCISES

1. Choose the appropriate subject pronoun.

Aimes-...... sortir ?
Les cartons d'invitation que ..... faites sont élégants.
Mon frère et moi ..... irons chez tes parents samedi.
Serait-..... déjà rentrée de sa soirée ?
Ici ..... se sent comme chez soi.

2. Complete the following sentences using appropriate disjunctive pronouns.

J'aime le cinéma. → Moi, j'aime le cinéma.
Nous aimons danser.
Elle s'amuse, mais il s'ennuie !
Ils vont dîner chez des amis.
Tu es amoureux !

3. Complete with the appropriate pronouns.

..... es souvent invité(e) chez des amis, ... ?
..... je ne sors jamais en semaine. ..... sortez, ... ?
....., elles ont de la chance, ... sont invitées partout.
Eh ! ..... là-bas, oui ....., ... avez votre carton d'invitation ?

KEY TO EXERCISES

1. tu - vous - nous - elle - on.
2. nous - elle / lui - eux - toi.
3. tu / toi - moi / vous / vous - elles / elles - vous / vous / vous.

HOW TO SAY IT !

INVITER QUELQU'UN :

– Je serais heureux de vous avoir à dîner, mercredi.
– Je vous invite à dîner, vendredi, à 20 h 30.
– Accepteriez-vous de déjeuner avec moi, mardi ?
– Venez prendre le thé, samedi.
– Si vous avez le temps, on prend un verre.
– Viens dîner samedi prochain, il y aura des copains.

– Je t'invite à une fête, samedi.

– Vous voulez nous accompagner ?

INVITING SOMEONE :

– I'd be happy if you came for dinner on Wednesday.
– I'd like to invite you for dinner on Friday, at 8.30 p.m.
– Would you like to have lunch with me, on Tuesday ?
– Come for tea on Saturday.
– If you have the time, let's have a drink.
– Come for dinner next Saturday, there'll be some friends (of mine).
– I'd like to invite you to a party on Saturday.
– Would you like to come with us ?

A very successful do !
(pincer = to pinch ; fesse = buttock)

Jeux

– Édouard ! Ça alors ! Il y a une éternité qu'on ne se voit plus ! Où étais-tu ?
– Eh bien, j'ai tout arrêté.
– Quoi, toi, tu ne joues plus ?
– Non, plus du tout.
– Mais tu gagnais tout le temps que ce soit aux cartes, à la roulette, au Loto. Tu avais toujours le chic pour trouver le bon numéro.
– Oui, ça marchait trop bien... Et le jour où j'ai gagné le plus gros lot de ma vie, je l'ai aussitôt rejoué et j'ai tout perdu. C'est la pire chose qui me soit jamais arrivée. C'est pour ça que j'ai décidé d'abandonner les jeux de hasard et de me reconvertir. Je travaille dans l'informatique à présent !

– Edouard ! Well, I never ! We haven't seen each other for ages. Where have you been ?
– Well, I gave it all up.
– What ! You ? You don't gamble any more ?
– No, not at all.
– But you used to win all the time, whether it was at cards, roulette or the Lottery. You always had the knack of finding the right number.
– Yes, it worked too well... And the day I won the biggest jackpot of my life, I immediately played it again and lost it all. It's the worst thing that has ever happened to me. That's why I decided to give up games of chance and turn to something else. Now I work with computers.

Gambling

BON À SAVOIR

Many French people like gambling and have a wide choice, ranging from the casino, where entry is controlled (evening dress compulsory, no previous incidents in the gaming world, over the minimum legal age...) to the "tiercé" for more modest budgets (betting on horse racing through the "Paris Mutuel Urbain" or "P.M.U." - the official bookmakers organisation). The racing results are announced each evening on the radio and TV and listed in daily newspapers, but punters also have their own newspapers, such as "Paris Turf".

Other games of chance such as "le Loto" (national lottery), "Tapis Vert" (betting on a sequence of four cards) and "Tacotac" (buying cards with, hopefully, the winning number) are also very popular.

More than 45 thousand million francs are spent on games of chance each year, earning 12 thousand million francs for the State (the equivalent of approximately 4% of total income tax revenue).

VOCABULARY

un casino	casino
un champ de courses	racecourse
un concours	competition
les échecs	chess
le flipper	pinball machine
la loterie	lottery
le tiercé	system of forecast betting
un cheval	horse
le gros lot	first prize, jackpot
un jeton	chip, token
un pari	wager
des résultats	results
la chance	luck
l'espoir	hope
le hasard	chance
la malchance	bad luck
acheter	to buy
deviner	to guess
gagner	to win
jouer	to play
miser	to stake
parier	to bet
perdre	to lose
tricher	to cheat

GRAMMAR

The imperfect

The imperfect expresses a repeated action in the past or an action which was in the process of happening at a particular moment in the past.
The endings : **-ais, -ais, -ait, -ions, -iez, -aient.**
The stem can be deduced from the forms used for the first person plural (« **nous** ») of the present tense.

*Nous gagnons → nous gagn**ions***

The superlative

The superlative is used to indicate intensity :

- **absolute : très** + adjective or adverb : *Il est très habile.*
  beaucoup (**de**) + noun : *Elle a beaucoup de chance.*
  verb + **beaucoup :** *Il joue beaucoup.*
- **relative : le plus/le moins**... (+ **de**) : *J'ai gagné **le plus** gros lot **de** ma vie.*

EXERCISES

1. Change to the imperfect.

Je joue souvent. → Je jouais souvent.

Il gagne plus qu'il ne perd. Nous préférons les jeux de cartes. Vous devinez souvent la bonne combinaison ? Quand ils sortent ensemble, ils boivent et jouent tout leur argent.

2. Change the following sentences using the superlative absolute (très or beaucoup).

Tu triches souvent. Elle joue aux cartes. Vous fréquentez les champs de courses ? Nous aimons les concours. Ils sont bons joueurs.

KEY TO EXERCISES

1. gagnait / perdait – préférions – deviniez – sortaient / buvaient et jouaient.
2. Tu triches très souvent. – Elle joue beaucoup aux cartes. – Vous fréquentez beaucoup les champs de courses ? – Nous aimons beaucoup les concours. – Ils sont très bons joueurs.

HOW TO SAY IT !

Dire sa surprise :

– C'est étonnant / surprenant !
– Ça m'étonne...
– Ça me surprend...
– Je suis surpris(e) / étonné(e).
– Quelle chance !
– C'est incroyable !
– Tant de malchance, c'est désespérant !
– Sans blague ! (familier)
– Je n'en reviens pas !
– Ça alors !
– Comment !
– Quoi !
– Tiens !
– Oh !

Expressing surprise :

– It's astonishing/surprising
– That astonishes me ...
– That surprises me ...
– I'm surprised/astonished.
– What luck !
– It's incredible !
– Such bad luck, it's hopeless !
– You're joking ! (familiar)
– I can't get over it !
– Well I never !
– What !
– What !
– Well !
– Oh !

I'm unlucky !
(bol = bowl/luck)

Madrid, le 6 juillet

Chère Florence,

À partir du 1er septembre prochain, je vais m'installer en France. À Lyon.

Je cherche à me loger le plus près possible du centre-ville. Un appartement de trois pièces me conviendrait très bien. Je ne voudrais pas payer un loyer trop élevé. Je sais que je peux m'adresser à une agence ou lire les petites annonces immobilières dans les journaux. Mais je suis pressée, et, de loin, ce n'est pas facile. Alors j'ai pensé que vous pourriez peut-être m'aider.

Merci d'avance.

Amicalement.

Carmen

Madrid, 6th July

Dear Florence,

As of 1st September this year, I'll be living in France, in Lyon.
I'm looking for somewhere to live as near as possible to the town centre. A three-roomed flat would suit me very well. I don't want to pay to much rent. I know that I could go to an agency or read the "flats to let" advertisements in the newspapers. But I'm in a hurry and, from a distance, it isn't easy. So I thought that you might, perhaps, be able to help me.

Thanking you in advance,

Best wishes,

Carmen

More French people now live in towns and cities than in the country.
Most of the population (which totalled 58 million in 1991) live in towns of more than 50,000 inhabitants. The number of people living in large cities (Paris, Lyon, Marseille) has stopped increasing but the suburbs around them are still growing.
Twelve million French people live in houses, 25 million live in flats as owners ("propriétaires") or tenants ("locataires"), including 12.7 million in "HLM" - or "habitation à loyer modéré", the equivalent of British council housing.
50 % of all French people dream of living in a house and the number of second homes ("résidences secondaires") has doubled since 1980.

VOCABULARY

une agence immobilière	estate agency
un bâtiment	building
un domicile	address, home
un immeuble	block of flats
une location	renting
une maison	house
une (co)propriété	co-ownership
une résidence	residence
un studio	one-room flat
une villa	detached house
un balcon	balcony
un escalier	stairs
un rez-de-chaussée	ground floor
une terrasse	terrace
un étage	floor
un garage	garage
un parking	car park
une boîte aux lettres	letter box
une cave	cellar
un gardien	caretaker
un locataire	tenant
habiter	to live in, occupy
(se) loger	to find accommodation
vivre	to live

GRAMMAR

▮ *The comparative :*

The comparative of adjectives is formed using :
– **plus... que** (+) : *Ce studio est plus cher que l'autre.*
– **moins... que** (–) : *Mon appartement est moins grand que le tien.*
– **aussi... que** (=) : *Votre cuisine est aussi belle que la mienne.*

▲ *C'est un bon gardien, il est meilleur que le tien.*

EXERCISES

1. Complete the following sentences using the comparative form.

Les loyers sont *(+ élevés)* à Paris qu'en province. Les logements sont *(– chers)* en banlieue que dans la capitale. Je paie un loyer *(+ cher)* que mes amis et pourtant mon appartement est *(= grand)* que le leur !

2. Match the questions and answers.

1 - Vous cherchez un logement ?
2 - Vous avez des appartements à louer ?
3 - Les charges sont en plus ?

a) Oui, je cherche un appartement.
b) Non, c'est un prix charges comprises.
c) Oui, nous en avons.

3. Transform the following sentences, introducing the comparative of superiority.

L'appartement est grand, pas le studio. → L'appartement est plus grand que le studio.

Le concierge est compréhensif, pas le propriétaire.
Se loger à Paris est difficile, pas en province.
L'ascenseur est pratique, pas les escaliers.
L'agence immobilière est efficace, pas les petites annonces.

KEY TO EXERCISES

1. plus élevés - moins chers - plus cher - aussi grand.
2. 1/a - 2/c - 3/b
3. Le concierge est plus compréhensif que le propriétaire. Se loger à Paris est plus difficile qu'en province. L'ascenseur est plus pratique que les escaliers. L'agence immobilière est plus efficace que les petites annonces.

HOW TO SAY IT !

PROPOSER :

– À vendre, grande maison, au bord de la mer.

– C'est un appartement très clair, propre, bien équipé et pas cher.

– À louer, beau studio, place Saint-Michel.

– Je pars au Canada pour un mois. Si ça t'arrange, je te prête mon deux pièces.

OFFERING :

– For sale : large house, by the sea.

– It's a flat with a lot of light, clean, well–equipped and not expensive.

– To let, attractive one-roomed flatlet, place Saint-Michel.

– I'm going to Canada for a month. If it's any help to you, I'll lend you my two-room flat.

I'll be glad when we move out of this poky little hole !
(Cage à lapins = rabbits hutch / small appartment)

Médecine

– Bonjour, madame ! Entrez.
– Bonjour, docteur.
– Qu'est-ce qui vous amène ?
– Eh bien ! ça fait quelques jours que j'ai de la fièvre, j'ai un peu mal à la gorge et je tousse.
– Bien. Nous allons voir ça... Respirez bien fort... Toussez. Ouvrez la bouche... Donnez-moi votre bras... Votre tension est trop basse et votre gorge un peu rouge et enflée.
– C'est grave ?
– Ne vous inquiétez pas. Je vous fais une ordonnance : vous allez prendre ce médicament pour faire baisser la fièvre, du sirop pour votre toux. Reposez-vous quelques jours et tout ira bien.
– Merci, docteur. Au revoir.

– Hello ! Come in.
– Hello, doctor !
– What brings you here ?
– Well, I've had a temperature for several days, my throat's a bit sore and I've got a cough.
– Okay, we'll have a look at that... Breathe deeply... Cough. Open your mouth... Give me your arm... Your blood pressure is too low and your throat is a little red and swollen.
– Is it serious ?
– Don't worry. I'll give you a prescription : you'll take this medicine to bring down your temperature, and some syrup for your cough. Rest for a few days and everything will be fine.
– Thank you, doctor. Good-bye.

Medicine

BON À SAVOIR

Many medicines can only be obtained from the chemist's ("pharmacie") on presentation of a doctor's prescription ("ordonnance"). Chemist's can easily be spotted by means of their sign : an illuminated green cross.
There is always at least one chemist's open in the town (even on Sundays and bank holidays). Its address is given on a notice displayed on the door (or in the window) of the other chemist's in the area.
In the event of emergency, you may go to the "service des urgences" (casualty department) of any hospital. Telephone the police station who will give you the address of a doctor. For serious cases, dial 15 to summon the **SAMU** *ambulance service (***SAMU** *= "Service d'Aide Médicale Urgente" or emergency medical service).*
Most French people are covered by the Social Security ("la Sécu") to which they pay contributions. In exchange, a certain percentage of their medical expenses is reimbursed. It is also possible to take out an insurance ("une mutuelle") which makes up the difference (this is voluntary).

VOCABULARY

le cœur	heart	**une piqûre**	injection
l'estomac	stomach	**une prise de sang**	blood test
le foie	liver	**un rendez-vous**	appointment
le sang	blood	**une urgence**	emergency
la tension	blood pressure	**avaler**	to swallow
une douleur	pain	**opérer**	to operate
un(e) malade	invalid	**(se) sentir**	to feel
un patient	patient	**soigner**	to treat, look after
un médecin	doctor	**souffrir**	to suffer
une pharmacie	chemist's	**soulager**	to relieve
un remède	remedy, medecine	**supporter**	to bear
l'hôpital	hospital	**vomir**	to vomit

GRAMMAR

The partitive article

It is used to indicate a certain quantity of something (like « some / any » in English)

	affirmative	negative
masculine	**du** or **de l'**	**ne … de**
feminine	**de la** or **de l'**	**ne … d'**

Je prends du sirop mais je ne prends pas d'alcool.

EXERCISES

1. Conjugate in the present tense.

Ce chirurgien *(opérer)* dans une clinique privée.
Je *(demander)* un rendez-vous pour quand ?
Tu *(avaler)* tous les médicaments à la fois ?
Nous *(soigner)* les patients de 14 à 19 heures.

2. Change into the plural.

Je tousse beaucoup. → Nous toussons beaucoup.

Ce médicament soulage.
Je ne supporte pas les prises de sang.
Tu te reposes beaucoup ?
Tu t'inquiètes pour Hélène.

3. Choose the appropriate partitive article (du, de la, de l', des).

Je préfère ne pas manger ..... sucre plutôt que de grossir.
Il y a ..... limonade ..... fromage et si tu veux ..... vin.
Le médecin me conseille de prendre ..... aspirine.

Key to exercises

1. opère – demande – avales – soignons.
2. Ces médicaments soulagent. – Nous ne supportons pas les prises de sang. – Vous vous reposez beaucoup ? – Vous vous inquiétez pour Hélène.
3. de – de la / du / du – de l'.

HOW TO SAY IT !

PARLER DE SA SANTÉ :

• QUAND ON NE VA PAS BIEN :

– Je suis fatigué(e)/crevé(e).
– Je me sens mal / pas bien du tout.
– Je suis souffrant(e), faible, épuisé(e).
– Je n'en peux plus.
– J'ai mal au ventre.
– Je ne supporte plus ce mal de dents.

• QUAND ON VA BIEN :

– Je vais très bien.
– Je suis en pleine forme.
– Je me sens très bien.

TALKING ABOUT ONE'S HEALTH :

• WHEN YOU ARE UNWELL :

– I'm tired / exhausted.
– I'm feeling bad / I don't feel at all well.
– I feel ill / weak / worn out.
– I'm all in.
– I've got stomach pains.
– I can't stand this toothache any longer.

• WHEN YOU ARE FEELING FINE :

– I'm very well.
– I'm on top form.
– I feel very well.

Poor man, he's kicked the bucket !
(Lit. : "He's broken his pipe")

– Et voici le bulletin météorologique d'Antoine Leblanc. Alors, Antoine, quel temps pour demain ?

– Bonne nouvelle, le temps va s'améliorer ! On enregistrera deux ou trois degrés supplémentaires chaque jour, ce qui devrait nous conduire à avoir des températures conformes aux moyennes saisonnières sur toute la France. Le soleil quant à lui reviendra demain dans les régions méditerranéennes, samedi sur la moitié sud et dimanche sur la moitié nord. Demain, le ciel sera très nuageux, les éclaircies provisoires et les averses fréquentes. Les températures seront un peu plus douces : de 18 à 20° sur la moitié nord et de 21 à 27° sur la moitié sud. Voilà. Vous savez tout, ou presque.

– And here's the weather forecast from Antoine Leblanc. Well, Antoine, what's the weather going to be like tomorrow ?

– Good news, the weather's going to improve ! We'll be seeing temperatures rising by two or three degrees every day, bringing them up to the seasonal average for France as a whole. The sun, for its part, will return tomorrow over the regions bordering the Mediterranean, spreading to the southern half of the country on Saturday and to the northern half on Sunday. Tomorrow, the sky will be very cloudy, with only brief sunny spells and frequent showers. Temperatures will be a little warmer : between 18 and 20° in northern France and between 21 to 27° in southern France. That's it. You know everything, or almost.

Talking about the weather is often a good way to start a conversation... as the French proverb tells us: "Parler de la pluie et du beau temps" – making small talk (lit.: Talking about the rain and the fine weather).
There's a weather forecast ("bulletin météorologique") on TV every day after the news (in the morning, at 1.30 p.m., at 8.30 p.m., 10.30 p.m. and 11 o'clock depending upon the channel). The same is true of the radio.
The weather forecast attracts the greatest number of viewers and the weathermen / women are among the most widely-recognised people in France. Each daily newspaper also prints a weather forecast.
Thanks to the use of satellite pictures, the forecasts are becoming increasingly accurate and, in France, also cover weather in the rest of Europe and Northern Africa.

VOCABULARY

le ciel	sky	**un baromètre**	barometer
la chaleur	heat	**un degré**	degree
une averse	shower, downpour	**une prévision**	forecast
le brouillard	fog	**une température**	temperature
le froid	cold	**un thermomètre**	thermometer
le givre	frost	**un anticyclone**	anticyclone
la neige	snow	**une dépression**	depression
un nuage	cloud	**une tempête**	storm
un orage	storm	**geler**	to freeze
la pluie	rain	**neiger**	to snow
le vent	wind	**pleuvoir**	to rain
le verglas	black ice	**souffler**	to blow

GRAMMAR

The gender of nouns : masculine and feminine :

- **le/un/l'** + a masculine singular noun.
  un climat - le ciel - l'orage
- **la/une/l'** + a feminine singular noun.
  une averse - la nuit - l'étoile
- **les/des** + a masculine or feminine plural noun.
  les températures - des nuages

Contracted forms of the definite article :

– **de + le = du :** *Le lever du soleil*
– **de + les = des :** *Le climat des pays*
– **à + le = au :** *Du Nord au Sud*
– **à + les = aux :** *Aux sommets des montagnes*

EXERCISES

1. Choose the appropriate word.

brouillard - chaud - pleuvoir

La dépression arrive par l'ouest : il va .....
On ne voit rien avec ce .....
Il fait souvent ..... en été.

2. Complete the following sentences using «du, des, au, aux ...»

Il y a du vent ..... sud de la Loire. Le brouillard ..... matin. Des Alpes ..... Pyrénées : de la pluie! La température ..... prochains jours sera basse.

3. Put into the singular.

Les orages sont violents. → L'orage est violent.

Il y a eu des giboulées hier. Les températures sont remontées. Les pluies des semaines passées vont cesser. Les bulletins des services météorologiques sont bons.

KEY TO EXERCISES

1. pleuvoir - brouillard - chaud.
2. au - du - aux - des.
3. Il y a eu une giboulée hier. La température est remontée. La pluie de la semaine passée va cesser. Le bulletin du service météorologique est bon.

HOW TO SAY IT !

DEMANDER LE TEMPS QU'IL FAIT :

– Quel temps fait-il là-bas ?

– Il fait bon/mauvais ?
– Tu as eu beau temps ?
– Quel temps faisait-il ?

ASKING WHAT THE WEATHER IS LIKE :

– What's the weather like down there ?
– Is the weather good/bad ?
– Did you have good weather ?
– What was the weather like ?

SE PLAINDRE (DU TEMPS) :

– J'ai horreur de la pluie.
– Il n'arrête pas de pleuvoir.
– Quel sale temps !
– Quel temps pourri !
– Ce temps, c'est déprimant.
– Quelle chaleur !
– Il fait lourd.

COMPLAINING (ABOUT THE WEATHER)

– I can't stand the rain.
– It never stops raining.
– What awful weather !
– What terrible weather !
– This weather's depressing.
– How hot it is !
– It's sultry weather.

It's freezing cold !
(canard = duck)

Info n° 5

J.-M. Charles / Rapho

Fromages CRÉPET-BRUSSOL

Two inseparable companions

Cheese

France boasts an incomparable number of different cheeses – more than 100 different sorts and 350 varieties of all shapes and sizes. Some of them, such as roquefort and camembert, enjoy international reputations. There are various different kinds of cheese : soft white cheese ("fromages frais" : petit suisse, demi-sel), cheese speads ("fromages fondus"), hard cheeses ("fromages à pâte pressée" : port-salut, gruyère) and matured cheeses ("fromages affinés" : camembert, roquefort, etc.). Cheese should be respected, eaten slowly and savoured along with a good wine!

Wine

Wine is not merely an agricultural produce, it is also a work of art! Each vintage ("cru") has its own distinctive personality and should be served and tasted with due respect for a certain set of rules. More than 25 associations for the glory of French wine have been created since 1920. The "Confrérie des Chevaliers du Tastevin" has taken the punning motto : *Jamais en vain, toujours en Vin* ("Never in vain, always with wine").

Some basic rules

Serving wine :

- "great" wines : bottles are served with the dust of the cellar still on them, held horizontally in a wicker basket.
- red wines are served "chambrés" (at room temperature) (from 15° to 18°);
- white and rosé wines are served chilled (from 5° to 12°).
- champagne and sparkling wines ("mousseux") are served slightly "frappés" (cooled slowly in a bucket of iced water).
- wines must harmonize with the dishes they are served with and respect a subtle progression during the course of the meal :

– *Oysters, fish :* white or sparkling wine;
– *First course :* light white or rosé;
– *White meat, poultry :* full-bodied red wine or an extra dry champagne;
– *Red meat, game, cheese :* vigorous red wine;
– *Sweet or dessert :* sweet or sparkling wine;
– *Fruit :* mellow wine, dry champagne.

Tasting wine :

- Smell the wine first of all, to appreciate its bouquet.
- Then drink the wine very slowly. Avoid water and cigarettes.

D'après *Le Nouveau Guide France,* G.Michaud, A.Kimmel, Hachette, 1990.

Ma chérie,

Je voudrais te décrire l'état du jardin en ce nouveau printemps : tu serais émerveillée de voir combien les nouvelles plantations de ton père sont une réussite. Je crois que côté fruits et légumes nous serons gâtés.

Quelle joie de respirer cet air pur ! Quand je pense que vous vivez dans la pollution, en permanence loin de la nature. Toi qui aimais tant la campagne : tu étais tellement heureuse ici. Enfin, c'est la vie !

Figure-toi que je viens de déloger un nid qu'avait installé un oiseau dans... le salon !

Bon, je te quitte en t'embrassant tendrement.

Ta maman qui t'aime.

My dear,

I'd like to describe what the garden is like this new springtime : you'd be amazed to see what a success your father's new plants are. I think that as far as fruit and vegetables are concerned, we're going to be spoiled.

What a joy is it to breathe this pure air ! When I think that you're living in (all that) pollution, far away from nature all the time. You who loved the country so much : you were so happy here. Well, that's life.

Imagine that I've just cleared out a nest that a bird had built in the sitting room !

Well, I'll leave you now with a kiss.

Much love from Mother.

Nature

BON À SAVOIR

On Sundays, many families go for walks in the forest or in the woods and parks not far from the town.

For those who like walking, there is a whole network of paths to be taken by ramblers ("sentiers de grande randonnée" : G.R.). Maps (IGN, Michelin) and guidebooks can easily be found in bookshops.

French people who have a house with a piece of land attached are fond of gardening (" le jardinage "). There are an estimated 22 million gardening enthusiasts in France.

All round the large cities you can still see small allotments ("parcelles de terrain") where the townspeople grow fruit and vegetables in their spare time.

VOCABULARY

la forêt	forest
un arbre	tree
un champignon	mushroom
une fleur	flower
une pelouse	lawn
une plante	plant
l'air	air
la campagne	country, countryside
l'écologie	ecology
l'environnement	environment
l'oxygène	oxygen
la pollution	pollution
un fleuve	river (major)
la mer	sea
la montagne	mountain
une rivière	river (minor)
jaune	yellow
marron	brown
vert	green
arroser	to water
cueillir	to pick, gather
jardiner	to do the gardening
jeter	to throw
se faner	to wilt

GRAMMAR

▌ *The imperfect :*

The endings : **-ais, -ais, -ait, -ions, -iez, -aient.**

Nous arrosions - Je cueillais.

▌ *The pluperfect :*

This past tense is used to describe an action which took place before another one.

It is constructed using the imperfect of « **être** » or « **avoir** » + the past participle (the rules of agreement are the same as those for the perfect tense).

C'était un nid qu'avait installé un oiseau.

EXERCISES

1. Change to the pluperfect.

Nous avons cueilli des fleurs. → *Nous avions cueilli des fleurs.*

Il est arrivé. L'oiseau s'est envolé. J'ai acheté un bouquet de fleurs. Tu as vu le jardin. La pollution a tué tous les poissons.

2. Put the first verb into the imperfect and the second into the pluperfect.

Ils ne *(pouvoir)* rien contre les mauvaises herbes qui les *(envahir)*. J'*(aimer)* le jardin où on *(cueillir)* des fleurs. Elle *(connaître)* tous les noms des champignons que nous *(ramasser)*. Tu te *(promener)* là où nos parents nous *(emmener)* souvent.

3. Translate.

Il ne faut pas arroser les plantes au soleil. Je suis comme les plantes, j'ai besoin de respirer beaucoup d'oxygène. Ses nouvelles plantations n'ont pas résisté au mauvais temps.

Key to exercises

1. Il était arrivé. L'oiseau s'était envolé. J'avais acheté un bouquet de fleurs. Tu avais vu le jardin. La pollution avait tué tous les poissons.
2. pouvaient / avaient envahis – aimais / avait cueilli – connaissait / avions ramassés – promenais / avaient emmenés.
3. You mustn't water your plants in the sun. I'm like the plants, I need to breathe lots of oxygen. His new plants haven't withstood the bad weather.

HOW TO SAY IT !

RÉDIGER UNE LETTRE PERSONNELLE, INTIME :	WRITING A PERSONAL LETTER
AU DÉBUT :	**TO BEGIN :**
Ma chérie / Mon chéri	*My dear.*
Mon cher Jacques, ma chère Alice	*My dear Jacques / Alice.*
À LA FIN :	**TO CONCLUDE :**
Toutes mes amitiés.	*Kindest regards.*
Amitiés.	*Regards.*
Amicalement.	*Regards.*
À (très) bientôt.	*See you soon.*
Je t'embrasse (très) fort.	*With much love from...*
Ton / ta... qui t'aime.	*With love from your...*
Bisous.	*Kisses.*
Grosses bises.	*Big kisses.*

We went off for a break.
(Lit. : "We put ourselves in the green")

– Je t'assure que la moitié de ce que dit Pierre est stupide.
– Tu dis ça premièrement parce que tu es jaloux, deuxièmement parce que tu ne comprends rien à ce qu'il raconte.
– Je te parie cent balles que j'ai raison. Je te préviens, j'ai plus d'une preuve.
– Ah bon ?
– Il prétend que le quart des Français sont des alcooliques tout simplement parce que le taux de fréquentation des cafés est très élevé !
– Tiens donc !
– Ça te suffit comme preuve de stupidité ?

– I promise you that half of what Pierre says is stupid.
– You say that firstly because you're jealous and secondly because you don't understand anything he's talking about.
– I bet you 100 francs that I'm right. I warn you, I have more than one example (piece of evidence).
– Oh yes ?
– He claims that one quarter of French people are alcoholics simply because the rate at which people frequent cafés is very high !
– Well, I never !
– Is that enough to prove his stupidity ?

BON À SAVOIR

*Every French citizen has a personal 13-digit national social security number ("numéro de sécurité sociale") which is also used as an identification number (when taking examinations, enrolling at the university, dealing with the administration, etc ...). It is built up in the following way: sex of the individual (1 for a man or 2 for a woman), year of birth (2 digits), month of birth (2 digits), administrative region or "département" of birth (2 digits), code of the borough or district ("commune") (3 digits); the last group of 3 digits corresponds to an identification number attributed by the National Statistics Institute (**INSEE**).*
A useful tip : if you're in the street in Paris with an odd number on your left, you will be facing the end of the street with the numbers increasing in front of you and decreasing behind you. Conversely, if you have an even number on your left, you will be facing the beginning of the street (lower numbers).

VOCABULARY

un chiffre	figure, number
une addition	addition
une division	division
une fraction	fraction
une multiplication	multiplication
une soustraction	substraction
une dizaine	about ten
une douzaine	dozen
une centaine	about one hundred
beaucoup de	a lot (of)
(un) peu (de)	a little
plusieurs	several
pair	even
impair	odd
quart	quarter
demi(e)	half
compter	to count
calculer	to calculate
additionner	to add up
ajouter	to add
déduire	to deduct
diviser	to divide
multiplier	to multiply
soustraire	to subtract

GRAMMAR

Numbers :

- **Cardinal numbers :** See the Grammar Summary for details.
  ▲ quatre-vingt**s** – quatre-vingt-un
  cent – cent un – deux cent**s** – deux cent deux.
- **Ordinal numbers :**
  Premier(ère) (1er/re) – deuxième (2e) – troisième (3e)...
  centième (100e) – millième (1 000e)...
- **Numeral adverbs borrowed from Latin :**
  premièrement → primo (1°)
  deuxièmement → secundo (2°)
  troisièmement → tertio (3°)
  quatrièmement → quarto (4°)

EXERCISES

1. Write out in full.

402 – 600 – 3 000 – 180 – 781 – 19 374.

2. Transform as in the example.

Premier → premièrement (primo)

quatrième – deuxième – neuvième – cinquième – dixième.

3. Translate.

J'habite au huitième étage d'une tour de quinze étages. Il a déjà dépensé les trois quarts de son salaire et on est à peine à la moitié du mois. Elle compte aussi vite qu'un ordinateur.

KEY TO EXERCISES

1. quatre cent deux – six cents – trois mille – cent quatre-vingts – sept cent quatre-vingt-un – dix-neuf mille trois cent soixante-quatorze.
2. quatrièmement (quarto) – deuxièmement (secundo) – neuvièmement – cinquièmement – dixièmement.
3. I live on the eighth floor of a fifteen-storey tower block. He has already spent three-quarters of his salary and we're scarcely half-way through the month. She counts as quickly as a computer.

HOW TO SAY IT !

POUR AFFIRMER AVEC FORCE :

- **J'affirme.**
- **Je peux vous assurer.**
- **Je te/vous promets.**
- **Promis.**
- **Je t'assure.**
- **Je te jure.**
- **Juré *(familier).***

ASSERTING SOMETHING FORCEFULLY :

- *I maintain...*
- *I can assure you...*
- *I promise you...*
- *It's a promise.*
- *I assure you.*
- *I swear to you.*
- *Honestly! (familiar)*

POUR NIER :

- **Sûrement pas !**
- **C'est sûr que non.**
- **Absolument pas.**

DENYING :

- *Surely not!*
- *Certainly not!*
- *Absolutely not!*

I made the right choice !
(Lit. : "I drew the lucky number")

Orientation (1)

«Salut Sophie, c'est Dominique, je t'appelle pour t'expliquer comment retrouver le restaurant dont je t'ai parlé l'autre jour.

C'est au 32 avenue Clemenceau. En sortant de la gare, tu prends le boulevard qui est devant toi, tu suis la direction «centre-ville». Puis tu tournes à la troisième rue à gauche, devant les grands immeubles en verre.
Lorsque tu verras, sur ta droite, une vieille maison (c'est là qu'habite Paul), tu trouveras au prochain carrefour l'avenue Clemenceau. Bon, j'espère avoir été clair.
Allez, à bientôt.

Salut !»

« Hello Sophie, it's Dominique. I'm calling to tell you how to find the restaurant I spoke to you about the other day.
It's at 32 avenue Clemenceau. As you leave the station you take the boulevard which is in front of you, and you follow the direction « centre-ville » (town centre). Then you take the third street on the left, in front of the tall glass buildings.
When you see an old house on your right (that's where Paul lives), you'll find avenue Clemenceau at the next crossroads. I hope that's clear.
See you soon.

Bye »

Direction (1)

28

BON À SAVOIR

Three French cities (Lyon, Marseille and Paris) are divided into "arrondissements" (numbered 1, 2, 3, etc.) but traditional parts of the city (or "quartiers") are still referred to by name: the Croix-Rousse and Fourvière in Lyon; the Vieux-Port and Cannebière in Marseille; the Champs-Elysées and the Quartier latin in Paris.
The front doors of many buildings in towns and cities are kept locked for security reasons and can only be entered by using a code or entry phone.
The address of a building is the same as its postal address.
The post code ("code postal") is a 5-digit number. The first two digits correspond to the number of the "département" (administrative region).

VOCABULARY

un immeuble	building
un village	village
une direction	direction
une distance	distance
après	after
avant	before
derrière	behind
devant	in front of
(à) droite	right
(à) gauche	left
le nord	north
le sud	south
l'est	east
l'ouest	west
un ascenseur	lift
un numéro	number
un code	code
un étage	floor, storey
un interphone	entry phone
aller	to go
habiter	to live in, occupy
indiquer	to indicate, show
(se) trouver	to find oneself
vivre	to live

Orientation (1)

GRAMMAR

▮ *The relative pronouns* qui, que, dont... :

- Subject : *L'homme* ***qui*** *est au bar.*
- Direct object : *L'homme* ***que*** *tu vois.*
- Object with the preposition **de :**
  L'homme ***dont*** *je te parle.*
- and also : **auquel, à laquelle, auxquels, auxquelles, où, quoi, lequel, duquel...**

▮ *Prepositions of place :*

Prepositions are used to link words in a sentence : « **à, au, dans, en, devant, derrière, jusque, sur, sous, près de, entre, vers** » ...

EXERCISES

***1. Transform the sentence using* qui, que *or* où.**

Voilà une ville ancienne. → Voilà une ville qui est ancienne.
Voilà, j'habite là. Voilà le parc, j'y vais souvent. Voilà mon livre, je t'en ai parlé. Voilà mon voisin, il travaille chez I.B.M.

***2. Choose the appropriate relative pronoun* où, qui *or* dont.**

Où – qui – dont.
C'est Dominique ..... écrit à Sophie. C'est la maison ..... habite Paul. Voici l'immeuble ..... je t'ai parlé. J'aime les maisons ..... sont anciennes. Je ne sais pas ..... aller.

3. Translate.

Pour aller au centre-ville, vous allez devant vous. Vous suivez les indications jusqu'au bout. C'est très près d'ici. Et derrière la cathédrale vous trouverez la poste et les commerces.

KEY TO EXERCISES

1. Voilà où j'habite. Voilà le parc où je vais souvent. Voilà le livre dont je t'ai parlé. Voilà mon voisin qui travaille chez IBM.
2. qui - où - dont - qui - où.
3. To get to the town centre, go straight ahead. Follow the directions to the end. It's very near here. And behind the cathedral you'll find the post office and the shops.

HOW TO SAY IT !

DEMANDER SON CHEMIN :

– Où est la poste ?
– Est-ce qu'il y a une banque par ici ?
– Est-ce que vous pourriez m'indiquer où se trouve... ?
– Comment aller à Bordeaux ?
– Est-ce que vous connaissez le centre commercial ?

ASKING THE WAY :

– Where's the post office ?
– Is there a bank here ?
– Could you tell me where... is ?
– How do I get to Bordeaux ?
– Do you know the shopping centre ?

INDIQUER SON CHEMIN À QUELQU'UN :

– Vous allez à droite.
– Continuez tout droit.
– Suivez cette rue puis tournez à gauche.
– Enfin prenez l'avenue...

TELLING SOMEONE THE WAY :

– You turn right.
– Carry on straight ahead.
– Take this street and then turn left.
– Then take the avenue.

Is that your pad ?
(crécher/crèche = crib/pad)

– Excusez-moi...
– Oui ?
– Je voudrais aller au commissariat de police mais je ne connais pas la ville.
– C'est très facile si vous êtes à pied, mais en voiture, c'est plus compliqué. Continuez tout droit jusqu'au deuxième feu ; là vous arrivez à un grand carrefour, vous le traversez, et vous marchez jusqu'à la troisième rue à gauche, vous faites encore cent mètres et vous y êtes.
– Merci beaucoup ! J'espère que je vais trouver !

– Excuse me ...
– Yes ?
– I'd like to go to the police station but I don't know the town.
– It's very easy if you're on foot, but it's more complicated by car. Go straight ahead as far as the second set of traffic lights ; there, you arrive at a large crossroads. Cross it and walk as far as the third road on the left. Go another hundred metres and you're there.
– Thanks a lot ! I hope I'll find it !

BON À SAVOIR

Roadsigns in the country and in towns are colour-coded:
- signs with a blue background indicate motorways and those with a green background indicate alternative routes (known as "touristiques" because they are more scenic than the motorway).
- Colour also indicates the type of establishment: yellow is used for post offices and red for fire stations.
- A signpost with the letter H indicates a hospital, while I denotes an information office ("bureau d'information" or "syndicat d'initiative"). The letter T is used for tourist offices.
If you need a chemist's, look out for the illuminated green cross above the shop.

VOCABULARY

un automobiliste	motorist
un cycliste	cyclist
un motard	motorcyclist
un piéton	pedestrian
un autobus	bus
une moto	motorcycle
une amende	fine
la chaussée	road (surface)
un trottoir	pavement
un feu (rouge/vert)	traffic light (red/green)
un horodateur	parking meter
un passage piétons	pedestrian crossing
un passage souterrain	subway
un sens unique	one-way street
un P. V.	parking ticket
un ticket	ticket
une voie	way, lane, track
autorisé	authorized
interdit	forbidden
payant	paying
(se) promener	to go for a walk
(se) garer	to park
stationner	to park
traverser	to cross (over)

GRAMMAR

Personal pronouns :

	Person	Direct object
singular	1st 2nd 3rd	**me** **te** **le, la, l'**

	Person	Direct object
plural	1st 2nd 3rd	**nous** **vous** **les**

If the verb begins with a vowel, the pronoun elides :
me → **m'** te → **t'** le, la → **l'**

▲ The direct object personal pronoun is placed before the verb except in the affirmative imperative :
Suis-nous ! Suis-moi ! (me → moi).

The gerund :

The gerund is formed using **en** + the present participle of the verb. It expresses an idea of simultaneity, of manner, means, cause, etc.

Je travaille en chantant.

EXERCISES

1. *Choose the appropriate word.*

passer – plan – renseignement – droit.

Demande-lui un ..... ! Il connaît le chemin. Sais-tu par où ..... ? Je cherche un ..... de la ville. Continue et va tout ..... !

2. *Use a direct object pronoun as shown in the example.*

Je regarde les panneaux. → Je les regarde.

Il voit sa sœur. – Elle emmène ses parents. – Vous lisez le plan.

3. *Answer the questions using a gerund.*

Comment tu vas là-bas ? (prendre) ma voiture. Quand l'as-tu vu ? (chercher) mon chemin. Comment trouver ? (lire) le guide.

KEY TO EXERCISES

1. renseignement – passer – plan – droit.
2. Il la voit. Elle les emmène. Vous le lisez.
3. en prenant – en cherchant – en lisant.

HOW TO SAY IT !

DEMANDER SON CHEMIN À QUELQU'UN :

– Pourriez-vous m'indiquer où se trouve la gare ?
– Pardon, vous pourriez me dire comment y aller ?
– Comment on fait pour aller au marché aux Puces ?
– J'y vais comment ?
– On y va comment ?

ASKING SOMEONE THE WAY :

– Could you tell me where the station is ?
– Excuse me, could you tell me how to get there ?
– How do you get to the flea market ?
– How do I get there ?
– How do you get there ?

DIRE QU'ON NE COMPREND PAS :

– Excusez-moi, je ne comprends pas !
– Est-ce que vous pourriez répéter doucement ?
– Désolé, je n'ai pas compris !

SAYING YOU DON'T UNDERSTAND :

– Excuse me, I don't understand !
– Could you repeat that slowly ?
– Sorry, I didn't understand !

Held up by a traffic jam !
(bouchon = cork/traffic jam)

– Bonjour, monsieur, je viens faire une déclaration de vol.
– Oui. Qu'est-ce qu'on vous a volé ?
– Mon autoradio.
– Ça s'est passé comment ?
– On a cassé la vitre de ma voiture.
– Je vois. Et votre voiture se trouvait où ?
– En stationnement devant chez moi.
– Vous avez les papiers du véhicule ?
– Oui. Tenez.
– Vous portez plainte ?
– C'est obligatoire ?
– Non. C'est comme vous voulez.
– Moi, je voulais juste une attestation pour me faire rembourser par mon assurance.

– Hello, constable, I've come to declare a theft
– Yes. What's been stolen ?
– My car radio.
– How did it happen ?
– They broke my car window.
– I see. And where was your car ?
– It was parked in front of my house.
– Do you have your car papers ?
– Yes. Here you are.
– Are you lodging a complaint ?
– Is it compulsory ?
– No, it's as you like.
– I would just like a certificate so that I can get reimbursed by my insurance company.

Police

30

BON À SAVOIR

There are several state organisations in charge of ensuring the security of the French territory and its citizens: the Customs ("les douanes"); the national police ("police nationale") which is under the responsibility of the Home Office ("ministère de l'Intérieur"); the "gendarmerie nationale" which is under the responsibility of the ministry of Defence ("ministère de la Défense").

The gendarmes are seen more in the country and in holiday areas (surveillance of beaches, etc.) than the regular police who operate in the cities. Some members of these forces work in special units - vice squad ("brigade mondaine" or "brigade des moeurs"), drug squad ("brigade des stupéfiants"), flying squad ("brigade volante"), etc.

In the case of accident or attack, telephone the police by dialling 17 or the fire brigade by dialling 18.

VOCABULARY

un commissariat	police station (cities)
la gendarmerie	police station (country/small towns)
police-secours	emergency service
le poste	post, police station
une amende	fine
une contravention	(parking) fine
un contrôle (d'identité)	(identity) check
un constat	report
un crime	murder, crime
un délit	offense, crime
une infraction	minor offense
une plainte	complaint
une enquête	investigation
la garde à vue	police custody
une arrestation	arrest
un rapport	report
une surveillance	surveillance
un agent	(police) officer
un commissaire	superintendent
un délinquant	delinquent
les gendarmes	policemen (country/small towns)
un(e) inspecteur(trice)	inspector
un(e) voleur(euse)	thief

GRAMMAR

▌ *The imperative present :*

The imperative is used to command, invite, request, advise (giving instruction).

Arrêtez-vous ! - Passez !

It only has three persons : **tu**, **nous** and **vous**.

The pronouns are not expressed except for the reflexive pronouns (in this case, the reflexive pronoun is placed after the verb, and « **tu** » becomes « **toi** »)

– Assieds-toi ! – Asseyez-vous !

EXERCISES

1. Put the verbs into the imperative in the person indicated. (Remember «tu» becomes «toi»).

(S'arrêter), s'il vous plaît. *(Conduire)* prudemment si tu veux éviter un accident. *(Aller)* au commissariat pour nos papiers. *(Finir)* vite ta déclaration. Cet homme est louche *(surveiller)*-le.

2. Put the verbs in brackets into the imperative. (Watch out for the person !).

Écouter / tu. Apprendre / nous. Travailler / vous. Se lever / tu. Sortir / nous.

3. As in the example, tell the person to do the following.

– à quelqu'un de téléphoner à la police. → Téléphonez à la police.

– à un ami de porter plainte.
– à un agent d'arrêter quelqu'un.
– à quelqu'un de faire attention.

KEY TO EXERCISES

1. Arrêtez-vous. – Conduis – Allons – Finis – Surveillez-le / surveille-le.
2. Écoute. – Apprenons. – Travaillez. – Lève-toi. – Sortons.
3. Porte plainte ! – Arrêtez-le ! – Faites attention !

HOW TO SAY IT !

DONNER DES ORDRES :

- **Arrêtez-vous !**
- **Garez votre véhicule !**
- **Vos papiers !**
- **Halte !**
- **Circulez !**
- **Ne traversez pas !**
- **Remplissez ce formulaire.**

GIVING ORDERS :

- *Stop !*
- *Park your vehicle !*
- *Your papers !*
- *Stop !*
- *Move on !*
- *Don't cross !*
- *Fill in this form.*

UN PEU D'ARGOT :

- **Fais gaffe, c'est interdit.**
- **Attention ! Il y a des flics.**
- **Elle s'est fait piquer.**
- **Ils ont fait un casse.**

SOME SLANG :

- *Watch out, it's prohibited.*
- *Watch out. The cops are there.*
- *She got caught.*
- *They did a break-in*

I'm getting out of the nick !
(taule = prison; tôle = sheet metal)

J.-L. Pasquier / Rapho

L'Opéra-Bastille

THE CINEMA

It is usual practice to tip the usherette 1 or 2 francs, despite the fact that her (or his) presence seems rather more ornamental than useful!

Note that cinema tickets are cheaper on Mondays, although young people (less than 18), students and senior citizens (over 60) enjoy special rates all the time. It is also possible to buy a "cinema card" for 6 films which works out cheaper than buying individual tickets.

New films are shown in "salles d'exclusivité", usually from 2 o'clock p.m. until midnight.

The cinemas change their films on Wednesdays and occasionally on Fridays for certain films.

As you would expect, all the daily newspapers list what films are showing that week and carry reviews of new films. It is also possible to find out about what's on via Minitel (dial 36 15 OFFI).

THE THEATRE

For the main theatres (Chaillot, Comédie française, Odéon...), you should book a fortnight ahead, day for day, at the theatre itself or at the FNAC (*FNAC Alpha :* reservations for the theatre, concerts, shows... in the following FNAC bookshops : *FNAC Forum :* 1, rue Pierre Lescot, 1st arrondissement, tel : (33) (1) 4041 40 00, open Monday 13.00 - 19.00 and from Tuesday to Saturday, 10.00 - 19.30 ; *FNAC Montparnasse :* 136, rue de Rennes, 6th arrondissement, tel. : (33) (1) 49 54 30 00. Alternatively, use the "Billetel" terminals or Minitel (dial 36 15 "Billetel").

Two theatre **kiosks** sell half-price tickets for plays and shows the same day. You'll find them at 15, rue de la Madeleine, 8th arrondissement, and in the RER station, Châtelet-Les Halles, in the 1st arrondissement (from Tuesday to Saturday, 12.45 - 19.00). You have to go there to find out what's available.

THE OPERA

Ballets are staged in the old opera house, the Palais-Garnier (place de l'Opéra), while lyrical works can be seen at the new Opéra-Bastille (place de la Bastille).

Le conseil municipal s'est réuni hier à 15 heures sous la présidence du maire, M. Duverger, qui a ouvert la séance.

Il a surtout été question de la préparation des prochaines élections législatives qui auront lieu dans quinze jours.

Monsieur le maire a précisé que les listes électorales étaient prêtes et que le scrutin se déroulerait à la mairie et aux bureaux de vote de l'école Jules-Ferry.

Les panneaux sont déjà en place dans la ville pour accueillir les affiches des candidats.

Rappelons que notre département élira quatre députés.

N'oubliez pas de demander votre carte d'électeur à l'hôtel de ville.

The town council convened yesterday at 3 p.m. and was chaired by the mayor, M. Duverger, who opened the session.

The principal question discussed was the preparation for the forthcoming general elections which will take place in a fortnight.

The mayor declared that the electoral lists were ready and that the ballot would be held in the town hall and in the polling booths at Jules Ferry school.

Signboards for the candidates' posters have already been set up in the town.

We remind you that our department will elect four deputies.

Don't forget to ask for your voter's card at the town hall.

BON À SAVOIR

Political life moves to the rhythm of local, regional and general elections ("elections locales, régionales et nationales").

At the local level, "conseillers" (councillors) are elected in each "commune" and the town council ("conseil municipal") is chaired by a mayor ("un maire"). The "canton" is a group of "communes" governed by a "conseil général" (general council).

"Députés", or MPs, are elected in each "département" by universal suffrage. They represent their regions at the National Assembly ("Assemblée nationale") in the Palais-Bourbon which, with the "Sénat" (which meets in the Palais du Luxembourg) comprise the French "Parlement".

The "Président de la République" is elected directly by all French citizens. He appoints the Prime Minister, head of the government (which comprises the ministers and the secretaries of state).

VOCABULARY

une commune	parish, borough	**le parlement**	parliament
un département	French administration region	**un parti (politique)**	(political) parti
une région	region	**un régime (politique)**	(political) régime
une république	republic	**le Sénat**	Senate
un élu	elected representative	**l'Assemblée nationale**	National Assembly
le suffrage (universel)	universal suffrage	**un député**	member of Parliament
un vote	vote	**un préfet**	prefect
un citoyen	citizen	**un président**	president
un gouvernement	government	**un sénateur**	un senator
une majorité	majority	**élire**	to elect
une opposition	opposition	**voter**	to vote

GRAMMAR

▌ *The subject of the verb :*

In the following sentences :

« On élit les conseillers municipaux. »
« Le président nomme le premier ministre. »

« On » is the subject of **« élit »**" (from the verb **« élire »**), **« le président »** is the subject of **« nomme »** (from the verb **« nommer »**). The verb agrees in person (1st, 2nd or 3rd) and in number (singular or plural) with its subject.

EXERCISES

1. Underline the subject of the verb in the following sentences.

Les électeurs ont élu les députés.
Dans la mairie, les conseillers discutent avec animation.
Voilà qu'arrive le maire.
Sont-elles allées à la réunion électorale ?

2. Conjugate the verb in the perfect tense.

Le président réunissait les ministres. → Le président a réuni les ministres.

Les élections ont lieu en avril.
Le premier ministre parle au Sénat.
Nous étudions la liste des candidats.
Vous votez pour qui ?

3. Provide suitable subjects for the following sentences.

Sont-..... allées à l'Assemblée nationale ?
Quand irez-..... à la mairie ?
..... aurons terminé lorsque ..... reviendras.
..... sont partis voter.
..... comprends mal ta position politique.

KEY TO EXERCISES

1. Les électeurs – les conseillers – le maire – elles.
2. ont eu lieu – a parlé – avons étudié – avez voté.
3. elles – vous – Nous / tu – Ils – Je.

HOW TO SAY IT !

DONNER SON AVIS :

– J'adhère totalement à cette politique.

– I totally support this policy.

– J'affirme qu'il / elle a raison.

– I maintain that he is right in saying that.

– Je suis certain que ses arguments sont bons.

– I am certain that his arguments are sound.

– Je crois à la victoire de ce parti.

– I believe that this party will win.

– Je pense que leurs idées sont dangereuses.

– I think that their ideas are dangerous.

S'OPPOSER :

DISAGREEING :

– Je ne suis pas d'accord avec ses récentes prises de position.

– I do not agree with his recent declarations (lit. «stands»).

– Je ne crois pas ces slogans très efficaces.

– I don't think these slogans are very effective.

– Nous devrions systématiquement les contrer.

– We should counter (their arguments) systematically.

It's six of one and half-a-dozen of the other.
(Lit. : "It's bonnet white and white bonnet")

Poste

– Bonjour. Je voudrais envoyer une lettre recommandée.

– Vous avez rempli le formulaire ?

– Euh ! non. Ils sont où ?

– Là, sur votre gauche, les imprimés blancs. N'oubliez pas d'inscrire le nom du destinataire et de l'expéditeur. Bien. C'est 17 francs.

– Je voudrais aussi dix timbres pour l'Algérie.

– Hello. I'd like to send a registered letter.

– Have you filled in the form ?

– Er, no ! Where are they ?

– Over there, on your left, the white printed forms. Don't forget to write the name of the addressee and of the sender. Fine. That's 17 francs.

– I'd also like ten stamps for Algeria.

Post office

The post office provides a variety of different services: the sale of stamps (ordinary or special editions), the conveying of mail (and parcels weighing up to 7 kilos), facsimile transmissions, the deposit and withdrawal of money using a banker's card, a postal order ("mandat") or a giro account ("compte chèque postal").
You can also buy stamps at a "tabac" (café with a red lozenge, selling stamps, cigarettes, etc...) and sometimes in museums and hotels.
The postal service is independent of the telephone service (France Télécom) but post offices do sell "télécartes" ('phonecards) and usually have several public telephones.
Yellow is the official colour of post office vans, letter boxes, etc.

VOCABULARY

un employé	clerk, employee
le facteur	postman
une boîte aux lettres	letterbox
un bureau	office
la poste restante	poste restante
une carte postale	postcard
un colis	parcel
le courrier	mail
un aérogramme	airmail letter
une télécopie	fax
un télégramme	telegram
une enveloppe	envelope
un mandat	postal order
un paquet	packet, parcel
le poids	weight
la queue	queue
un reçu	receipt
un tarif	price list, rate
normal	ordinary
rapide	fast, express
réduit	reduced
envoyer	to send
poster	to post

GRAMMAR

▌*The plural of nouns :*

To form the plural of nouns, add :
- the letter « **s** » : *lettres, imprimés ...*
- the letter « **x** » for most words ending in **- au**, **-eau**, **-eu :** *des bureaux*

▲ *un journal → des journaux ; un cheval → des chevaux ; un travail → des travaux.*

▌*Envoyer :*

An irregular 1st conjugation verb in the present indicative : « **envoyer** »

J'envoie, tu envoies, il/elle envoie, nous envoyons, vous envoyez, ils/elles envoient.

EXERCISES

1. Put into the plural.

Est-ce que tu as une enveloppe ? → Est-ce que tu as des enveloppes ?

Ils affichent tout sur leur tableau. J'ai acheté un timbre où il y a un magnifique bateau. Poste-moi ce journal !

2. Conjugate the following verbs in the present indicative.

Nous vous *(envoyer)* toutes les informations dès que possible. Il *(coller)* son timbre sur l'enveloppe. Tu *(préférer)* envoyer ta carte postale comme ça, ou tu la *(mettre)* sous enveloppe ?

3. Translate.

Quel est le tarif d'une lettre pour l'Angleterre, s'il vous plaît ? Est-ce qu'il y a du courrier pour moi ? On m'a envoyé un paquet il y a un mois et je ne l'ai toujours pas reçu.

KEY TO EXERCISES

1. leurs tableaux - des timbres / de magnifiques bateaux - ces journaux.
2. envoyons - colle - préfères / mets.
3. What's the price of a letter to England, please ? Is there any mail for me ? I was sent a parcel one month ago and I still haven't received it.

HOW TO SAY IT !

POUR DIRE CE QU'ON VEUT :

– Donnez-moi cinq timbres au tarif normal.
– Il me faudrait dix timbres à tarif réduit.

SAYING WHAT YOU WANT :

– Give me five standard rate stamps.
– I need ten cheap rate stamps.

POUR DEMANDER LE PRIX :

– C'est combien ?
– Ça coûte combien ?
– Vous pourriez me dire combien ça coûte ?
– Je vous dois combien ?
– Quel est le prix d'un carnet de timbres, s'il vous plaît ?

ASKING THE PRICE :

– How much is it ?
– How much does it cost ?
– Could you tell me how much it costs ?
– How much do I owe you ?
– What is the price of a book of tickets, please ?

They always keep you waiting at the post office !
(poireau = leek ; poireauter = to be left kicking one's heels)

– Qu'est-ce que tu achètes comme journaux ?
– Un quotidien le matin en partant travailler ; de temps en temps, un journal régional pour les nouvelles locales et les faits divers ; selon l'humeur du moment un hebdo ou un mensuel ; un magazine de décoration ou de jardinage pour ma femme ; des bandes dessinées pour les enfants...
– Et tu réussis à tout lire ?
– Pas vraiment, je regarde la « une » et je parcours les éditoriaux et les titres, je choisis les articles qui m'intéressent. Pour les périodiques, je lis seulement certaines rubriques. Je n'ai pas le temps de lire de A à Z.

– What newspapers do you buy ?
– A daily in the morning when I leave for work ; a regional paper from time to time for local news and events and, depending on how I feel, a weekly or a monthly ; a decoration or gardening magazine for my wife ; comics for the children.
– And you manage to read them all ?
– Not really. I read the front page and glance through the editorials and headlines, I choose the articles which interest me. As for the magazines, I just read certain sections. I don't have the time to read from A to Z.

BON À SAVOIR

The most popular dailies :
- the principal national papers (published in Paris but also distributed in the provinces) : Le Figaro, Le Monde, Le Parisien, France-soir, L'Équipe (specialising in sports news), Libération (Libé), L'Humanité, La Croix ;
- the principal regional papers (these may also be distributed in Paris) : Ouest-France, La Voix du Nord, Sud-Ouest, Le Progrès, Le Dauphiné libéré, La Nouvelle République du Centre-Ouest, Nice-Matin, La Montagne, L'Est-Républicain, La Dépêche du Midi ;
- the principal weeklies : L'Express, Le Point, Le Nouvel Observateur (L'Obs), L'Événement du Jeudi, Le Canard enchaîné (satirical newspaper), Le Nouvel Economiste.
You can buy papers and magazines in kiosks and bookshops/stationer's ("librairie-papeterie"), in stations and airports and in certain large stores. Foreign papers are found mainly in the large cities. They can also be obtained by special order or by subscription. There are also local papers which are distributed free. They contain mainly classified ads.

VOCABULARY

un(e) lecteur(trice) reader
un(e) rédacteur(trice) sub-editor
une rédaction editorial staff
une (petite) annonce (classified) advertisement
une colonne column
une rubrique column, section
un reportage report
un format format
une page page
la publicité advertising
un abonnement subscription
la distribution distribution
un kiosque (à journaux) (newspaper) kiosk
une parution publication, appearance
un tirage (gros/faible) circulation (large/small)
un hebdo(madaire) weekly magazine
(s')abonner to take out a subscription

GRAMMAR

▮ *Formation of the gerund :*

The gerund is formed with **en** + stem of the verb + **ant** (the stem of the verb is obtained from the 1st person plural of the present indicative).

Verb **manger** → **nous mange/ons** → **en mangeant.**

It indicates that an action is taking place at the same time as another one. (The subject is the same for both verbs.)

Je le fais ***en partant.*** *→ Je le fais lorsque je pars.*
Je lis ***en écoutant*** *de la musique. → Je lis et j'écoute de la musique en même temps.*

EXERCISES

1.Choose the appropriate word.

tirage – lecteurs – annonces – format

Ce journal est très lu ; il a un ..... important. J'aime les journaux qui ont un petit ....., c'est pratique. Lis les petites ..... pour trouver un appartement. Le courrier des ..... est fascinant.

2. Transform by using the gerund as shown in the example.

J'ai trouvé cette annonce quand j'ai parcouru le journal. → J'ai trouvé cette annonce en parcourant le journal.

Achète le journal quand tu sors. Ne lis pas quand tu manges. Il regarde la télé et il lit son journal en même temps.

3. Translate.

Elle achète son journal en partant. On parle des articles intéressants en travaillant. Ce magazine a un gros tirage.

KEY TO EXERCISES

1. tirage – format – annonces – lecteurs.
2. Achète le journal en sortant. – Ne lis pas en mangeant. – Il regarde la télé en lisant son journal. / Il lit son journal en regardant la télé.
3. She buys her newspaper when she leaves. We talk about the interesting articles while we work. This magazine has a large circulation.

HOW TO SAY IT !

COMMENT RÉDIGER UNE PETITE ANNONCE :

• POUR VENDRE :

☐ Collections B.D. [bandes dessinées] et polars [romans policiers] à vendre – prix intéressant.

☐ Vends appt [appartement] neuf – 3 pièces – 80 m² – plein sud – cuisine équipée – Excellente affaire.

• POUR ACHETER :

Cherche meubles anciens – Étudierais toutes propositions. Contacter le journal.

DRAFTING A SMALL AD :

• SELLING :

☐ *Collection of comic strips and thrillers for sale – attractive price.*

☐ *Flat for sale : new – 3 rooms – 80 square metres – facing south – fitted kitchen – a bargain.*

• BUYING :

Antique furniture wanted – All offers considered. Contact the newspaper.

Let's see what they have to say in this rag.
(feuille de choux = cabbage leaf / newspaper)

Religion

La France est un pays de tradition judéo-chrétienne. Dominée d'abord par le catholicisme (dont les grandes dates rythment toujours le calendrier national), elle a vu s'installer – parfois non sans drames – le protestantisme, la religion israélite et, plus récemment, elle a accueilli l'islam.

Le catholicisme compte beaucoup moins de pratiquants que jadis. En revanche, les musulmans et les israélites, bien que minoritaires, sont devenus très actifs et observent scrupuleusement leur religion.

France is a country with a Judaeo-Christian tradition. Dominated first of all by Catholicism (whose main festivals still punctuate the national calendar), it has seen the arrival – not without tragedy at times – of Protestantism, the Jewish faith and, more recently, it has welcomed Islam.

The Roman Catholic church numbers far fewer regular churchgoers than in the past. In contrast, Muslims and Jews, in spite of being minorities, have become very active and strictly abide by their religion.

Half of the public holidays in France correspond to festivals of the Catholic Church :
- "Noël" : the Birth of Christ (25 December) (Christmas). "Pâques" : the Resurrection of Christ (March or April) (Easter). "Ascension" : the Ascension of Christ into heaven (May) (Ascension Day). "Pentecôte" : the descent of the Holy Spirit on the apostles (May or June) (Whit Sunday). "Assomption" : the taking up of the Virgin Mary into heaven (15 August) (Assumption). "Toussaint" : festival to honour all the saints (1st November) (All Saints' Day).
Before the Revolution in 1789, France was divided up into "paroisses" (parishes), each with its church and parish priest ("église et curé"). The parish still exists but has lost most of its administrative importance to the "commune". France is particularly rich in catholic churches and cathedrals and boasts many architectural beauties... but there are also many protestant churches ("temples"), synagogues ("synagogues") and mosques ("mosquées") in the larger cities for people of other confessions.

VOCABULARY

le christianisme	Christianity
l'islam	Islam
le judaïsme	Judaism
le baptême	baptism
une cérémonie	ceremony
la messe	mass
un sacrement	sacrement
une chapelle	chapel
une église	church
un(e) croyant(e)	believer
un(e) fidèle	believer, faithful
un pasteur	minister
un curé	parish priest
un prêtre	priest
un rabbin	rabbi
pratiquer	to be a churchgoer
prier	to pray
croire	to believe

Religion

GRAMMAR

■ ***The past participle :***

The main forms : masculine singular : **é, i, is, it, u;** feminine singular : **ée, ie, ise, ite, ue.** The past participle may be used as an adjective (agreeing with the noun it qualifies) or to form compound tenses.
The past participle then agrees :
– with the subject of the auxiliary « **être** » :
*Les hommes du XVe siècle étaient **attirés** par la religion. (masculine plural)*
– with the direct object of the auxiliary « **avoir** » only when it is placed before the past participle :
*Les religions que nous avons **connues**.* (feminine plural)

EXERCISES

1. Put into the perfect tense.

Nous connaissons cette église. → Nous avons connu cette église.
Les associations reçoivent les programmes annuels des cultes.
Les religions permettent de réaliser de grandes œuvres d'art.
Ce sont les prières que vous apprenez ?
Ils retirent leurs chaussures et ils rentrent.

2. Make the past participle (in brackets) agree in number and gender where necessary.

Vous avez assisté à la messe, dimanche ? Voilà la Bible que je vous ai promis. Elles ont reçu la visite du rabbin. Ces lignes sont lu par des milliers de personnes.

3. Match the following.
église → catholique

1. temple
2. rabbin
3. messe
4. mosquée
5. cathédrale

a) catholique
b) protestant
c) musulman
d) gothique
e) israélite

KEY TO EXERCISES
1. ont reçu *(recevoir)* – ont permis *(permettre)* – avez apprises *(apprendre)* – ont retiré *(retirer)* / sont rentrés *(rentrer)*.
2. assisté – promise – reçu – lues.
3. 1.b – 2.e – 3.a – 4.c – 5.d.

HOW TO SAY IT !

DIRE CE QUE L'ON CROIT. AFFIRMER SES CROYANCES RELIGIEUSES :

SAYING THAT YOU BELIEVE. ASSERTING YOUR RELIGIOUS BELIEFS :

- **Je crois en Dieu, en l'Église.** – *I believe in God, in the Church.*
- **Je suis croyant(e).** – *I'm a believer.*
- **Il faut aimer son prochain.** – *You must love your neighbour.*
- **Il / Elle est pratiquant(e).** – *She's a practising (Christian / Jew / Muslim ...)*
- **Je respecte la tradition / les règles de ma religion.** – *I respect the tradition/the rules of my religion.*

Look, a proper Holy Joe !
(grenouille = frog ; bénitier = font)

– Allô ! Bonjour, Anne, c'est Sophie.
– Salut ! ça va ?
– Oui, excuse-moi de te déranger mais... est-ce que tu aurais le numéro de téléphone de Philippe ?
– Oui, je crois. Attends... voilà : c'est le 46 62 10 10.
– Merci. Au fait, tu vas chez lui vendredi soir ?
– Oui.
– Comment on y va déjà ?
– C'est facile, mais tu ne veux pas qu'on y aille ensemble ? Ça sera plus sympa. Je passe te prendre à 8 heures.
– D'accord. Allez, à vendredi.

– Hello ? Hello, Anne. It's Sophie.
– Hi ! How are things ?
– Yes. I'm sorry to disturb you, but... would you (happen to) have Philippe's telephone number ?
– Fine, I think so. Hang on ... here it is : it's 46 62 10 10.
– Thanks. By the way, are you going to his place Friday evening ?
– Yes.
– How do you get there ?
– It's easy, but don't you want us to go there together ? It will be more friendly. I'll come to fetch you at 8 o'clock p.m.
– Alright. Well then, see you on Friday.

When you arrive in France, you can obtain information at the information desk in the airport or railway station. Look for the sign bearing the symbol i (for "information").
During opening hours (generally 8 a.m. to 12 noon and 2 - 4 p.m.), you can also obtain practical information from the tourist office, the town hall or the local police station about such things as directions to the nearest post office or bank, finding your way around the city, finding accommodation, etc.
If you're lost, don't hesitate to ask a police officer (they always have a street map in their pockets), a shopkeeper or a passerby for directions. Street maps can frequently be found on advertising boards on the pavement. In Paris, use the **SITU** *machines (you just type in your destination and the directions appear on a screen) or the maps posted up in all metro stations.*

VOCABULARY

l'accueil	reception
un formulaire	form
une indication	directions
une information	information
une précision	further detail
une question	question
la réception	reception
un sondage	(opinion) poll
le syndicat d'initiative	tourist information office
la mairie	town hall
un tuyau	tip (information) pipe
appeler	to call
chercher	to look for
connaître	to know
demander	to ask (for)
donner	to give
enquêter	to inquire, investigate
expliquer	to explain
(s')informer	to inquire
interroger	to question
(se) renseigner	to make inquiries
savoir	to know
s'excuser	to apologize
trouver	to find

GRAMMAR

■ ***The imperative of reflexive verbs :***

With reflexive verbs (« **se** » + verb), a reflexive pronoun is placed after the verb.

Se renseigner → *Renseigne-toi !*
Renseignons-nous !
Renseignez-vous !

▲ Négative → *Ne te renseigne pas !*
Ne nous renseignons pas !
Ne vous renseignez pas !

EXERCISES

1. Put the verbs into the imperative in the person indicated.

(se préparer, nous) pour partir.
(se présenter, vous) au commissariat.
(se renseigner, tu) par téléphone.

2. Put the sentences into the imperative.

Tu dois te présenter au bureau de renseignements. → Présente-toi au bureau de renseignements.

Il faut te calmer.
Il faut que nous nous informions.
Vous devriez vous renseigner.

3. Put the verbs into the imperative and add the negative.

(demander, vous) tous les catalogues.
(s'informer, toi) trop tôt, les horaires changent fin mai.
(interroger, nous) n'importe qui dans la rue.
(appeler, vous) les pompiers pour rien.
(se renseigner, toi) dans cette agence.

KEY TO EXERCISES

1. Préparons-nous... – Présentez-vous... – Renseigne-toi...
2. Calme-toi. Informons-nous. Renseignez-vous.
3. Ne demandez pas... – Ne t'informe pas... – N'interrogeons pas... – N'appelez pas... – Ne te renseigne pas...

HOW TO SAY IT !

Demander un renseignement :

– Dites-moi, où je peux changer de l'argent.
– Où se trouve la poste, s'il vous plaît ?
– Avez-vous l'heure ?
– Quelle heure est-il ?
– Quel jour sommes-nous ?
– Tu peux me donner le numéro de téléphone de... ?
– L'adresse de la banque, c'est bien ... ?
– Pardon, où se trouve la station de métro ?

Asking for information :

– (Could you) tell me where I can change money ?
– Where's the post office, please ?
– Do you have the time ?
– What time is it ?
– What day is it ?
– Can you give me (somebody's) phone number ?
– The address of the bank is (number, street), isn't it ?
– Excuse me, where's the underground station ?

I'll give you a hot tip.
(tuyau = pipe/tip)

Palais des Papes – Festival d'Avignon

Théâtre d'Orange ➤

FESTIVALS AND LOCAL CELEBRATIONS

To find out when and where the different festivals are being held, contact l'Association nationale de la diffusion culturelle : 5, rue Bellart, 75015 Paris, tel. : (33) (1) 47 83 33 58 or the local tourist information offices.
Another way of discovering France and the history of its inhabitants is to attend the local festival held every year, sometimes with parades in traditional costumes or cultural / sporting events.
Note that these festivals go under different names according to the region : fête votive, vogue (south-east), kermesse (north), fest-noz (Brittany), fête foraine, fête patronale, assemblée (Normany, Poitou).

Other theatre and music festivals are held during the summer for the most part. Some of the more famous are : le festival de Paris (music), le festival d'Avignon (theatre), le festival d'Aix-en-Provence (classical music).

There are three major cinema festivals held in the provinces : Cannes, Deauville (American films), Avoriaz (horror films and science fiction)...

Salutations

– Tiens, voilà Sylviane ! Sylviane !

– Oh ! bonjour Paul !

– Sylviane, je te présente Thierry.

– Enchantée.

– Tu sais, c'est mon ami qui habite en Bretagne et qui est informaticien.

– Ah oui ! Paul m'a beaucoup parlé de toi.

– Et moi donc ! Je suis vraiment content de faire ta connaissance. Et toi, tu fais quoi au fait ?

– Je suis médecin à l'hôpital Ambroise-Paré.

– Et si on allait prendre un verre pour continuer les présentations ?

– D'accord !

[illegible] l'hôpital Ambroise-Paré [illegible]

– Oh look, there's Sylviane ! Sylviane !

– Oh ! Hello Paul !

– Sylviane, meet Thierry.

– Delighted.

– You know, he's the friend of mine who lives in Brittany and who's a computer technician.

– Oh yes ! Paul has spoken about you a lot.

– Me too ! I'm really pleased to meet you. And what in fact do you do ?

– I'm a doctor at the Ambroise-Paré hospital.

– And what if we had a drink to get to know one another better ?

– Alright !

BON À SAVOIR

You can greet someone with "bonjour" (hello) at any time of the day.
"Bonsoir" (good evening) can be used instead of "bonjour" from late afternoon onwards.
"Bonne nuit" (good night) is more often used between members of the same family, just before going to bed.
The French frequently use greetings referring to people's health: "Ca va ?" "Comment ça va ?" "Comment allez-vous ?"(How are you ?). The usual answer is "Ça va. Merci. Et toi / vous ?"
When greeting or taking leave of one another, members of the same family, friends, school friends and even colleagues will kiss one another on the cheek 2, 3 or even 4 times depending on the region.they come from originally.

VOCABULARY

content(e)	pleased
enchanté(e)	enchanted
agréable	pleasant
timide	shy
connu(e)	known
la politesse	politeness, courtesy
un nom	name
une poignée de main	handshake
un prénom	first name
une profession	profession
une carte de visite	visiting card
dire bonjour	to say hello
dire au revoir	to say goodbye
serrer la main	to shake hands
ressembler	to look like
vouvoyer	to address sb using «vous»
tutoyer	to address sb using «tu»
présenter	to introduce
s'appeler	to be called
s'embrasser	to kiss
se présenter	to introduce oneself
arriver	to arrive
connaître	to know

GRAMMAR

Possessive adjectives :

• Possessive adjectives agree : in person with the possessor ; in gender and number with the object possessed :

	1 object		several objects
	masculine	feminine	plural
1 possessor	mon ton son	ma ta sa	mes tes ses
several possessors	notre votre leur		nos vos leurs

• Possessive pronouns (which obey the same rules of agreement as possessive adjectives) remplace ;

	1 object		several objects	
	masculine	feminine	masculine	feminine
1 posessor	le mien le tien le sien	la mienne la tienne la sienne	les miens les tiens les siens	les miennes les tiennes les siennes
several possessors	le nôtre le vôtre le leur	la nôtre la vôtre la leur	les nôtres les vôtres les leurs	

EXERCISES

1. Complete with the appropriate possessive adjective **(mon, ma, mes ...).**

..... hommages, chère madame. C'est ..... carte de visite, Paul ? Je vous présente ..... enfants. Je n'ai pas reçu de ..... nouvelles. Il leur a présenté ..... famille.

2. Answer as in the example.

C'est sa carte de visite ? → C'est la sienne.

C'est mon voisin ? Ce sont nos affaires ? Ce sont leurs amis ? C'est ta voisine ?

KEY TO EXERCISES

1. mes - ta - mes - vos/tes - sa.
2. C'est le mien. Ce sont les nôtres. Ce sont les leurs. C'est la mienne.

HOW TO SAY IT !

COMMENT PRENDRE CONGÉ :

– Au revoir !
– Salut !
– À bientôt !
– À plus tard !
– À tout à l'heure.
– À la semaine prochaine.
– (Allez) bonne journée !
– Bon après-midi !
– Bonnes vacances !
– Bonsoir !
– Allez, bonne chance !
– À très bientôt !

HOW TO TAKE LEAVE :

– Goodbye !
– Cheerio !
– See you soon !
– See you later !
– See you in a moment !
– See you next week.
– (Well) have a good day !
– Good afternoon !
– Have a good holiday !
– Good evening !
– Well, good luck !
– See you before long !

Everything okay, then ?
(rouler = to roll/go well)

« Le mois dernier, lorsqu'on a décidé d'aller au théâtre, on a fait les réservations par téléphone ; heureusement, il y avait encore quelques places, et mon mari est passé prendre les billets deux jours plus tard.

Par contre, lundi dernier, quand on est allé au cinéma, il y avait une queue monstre, et on a attendu dehors plus d'une demi-heure, sous la pluie !

Du coup, pour le concert du prochain festival, en juillet, on a déjà réservé. Bref, quand on s'y prend à temps, on est tranquille ! »

« Last month, when we decided to go to the theatre, we made the reservations by telephone. Fortunately, there were still a few seats and my husband went in to get the tickets two days later.

On the other hand, when we went to the cinema last Monday, there was an enormous queue and we waited outside for more than half an hour, in the rain!

As a result, for the concert in the forthcoming festival in July, we've already reserved. In a word, when you do things in time, you can rest easy. »

BON À SAVOIR

Cinema programmes usually change on Wednesdays. In Paris, all information relating to cultural events in the capital and its suburbs (cinemas, theatres, concerts, exhibitions, museums, etc.) can be found in magazines such as L'Officiel des Spectacles, Pariscope, 7 à Paris or Télérama.
In the provinces, the programmes appear in the local newspaper.
Festivals take place throughout the year all over France : music (Aix-en-Provence), theatre (Avignon), cinema (Cannes, Deauville, Avoriaz)... It's worth knowing that cinema tickets are cheaper on Mondays while old age pensioners and students enjoy reduced rates all week.

VOCABULARY

un(e) acteur(trice)	actor
un(e) chanteur(teuse)	singer
un(e) comédien(ne)	actor
un(e) danseur(euse)	dancer
un chef d'orchestre	conductor
un metteur en scène	producer, film director
une mise en scène	production
un décor	scenery
un écran	screen
un fauteuil	seat
un film	film
un guichet	ticket office
une place	seat
le programme	programme
un cabaret	cabaret
un café-théâtre	theatre workshop
le cirque	circus
un concert	concert
un opéra	opera
un orchestre	orchestra
une pièce	play
une soirée	evening performance
applaudir	to applaud
jouer	to play, act, show (film)
réserver	to book

GRAMMAR

■ *The position of the adverb with the perfect tense :*

The adverb is placed between the auxiliary (« **avoir** » or « **être** » in the appropriate form) and the past participle.

*Nous sommes **déjà** allés le voir.*
*Il a **mal** joué.*
*Il est **toujours** parti.*
▲ *Elle **n'**a **pas encore** fini.*

EXERCISES

1. Choose the appropriate word.

place – dirige – queue – billets – réservé.

As-tu pris les ..... pour ce soir ?
Il y a encore de la ..... au dernier rang.
Qui ..... l'orchestre ?
Il faut faire la ..... dehors.
Tu as ..... des places ?

2. Change as in the example.

J'ai vu ce film. / Souvent ? → Oui, j'ai souvent vu ce film.

Nous avons eu des places. / Toujours ?
J'ai écouté cet opéra. / Déjà ?
On est allé le voir. / Souvent ?
Il a joué. / Mal ?

3. Translate.

Le décor de la pièce qu'on a vue était superbe.
Cet acteur a souvent reçu des récompenses.
Tu connais ce chef d'orchestre ?

KEY TO EXERCISES

1. billets – place – dirige – queue – réservé.
2. Oui, nous avons toujours eu des places. Oui, j'ai déjà écouté cet opéra. Oui, on est souvent allé le voir. Oui, il a mal joué.
3. The scenery of the play we saw was superb. That actor has often received awards. Do you know this conductor ?

HOW TO SAY IT !

COMMENT DEMANDER S'IL RESTE DES PLACES :

– Est-ce qu'il reste des places pour ce soir ?
– Avez-vous encore des places ?
– Il vous reste quelque chose ?

ASKING IF THERE ARE ANY SEATS LEFT :

– Are there any seats left for this evening ?
– Do you still have any seats ?
– Do you have anything left ?

COMMENT RÉSERVER UNE PLACE :

– Je voudrais faire une réservation pour le concert, s'il vous plaît.
– J'aimerais réserver pour ce spectacle.
– Est-ce qu'il serait possible de faire une réservation pour ce voyage et cet hôtel ?

RESERVING A SEAT :

– I'd like to make a reservation for the concert, please.

– I'd like to reserve for this show.
– Would it be possible to make a reservation for this trip and this hotel ?

That show will be a roaring success !
(Lit. : make a tobacco)

CLUB DES QUATRE VENTS

Stage d'été du 1er au 15 juillet

Lieu : Lozère.

La campagne et de nombreuses possibilités d'activités sportives : escalade, nautisme, cyclisme, équitation, tennis, jeux d'équipe, etc., sous la direction de moniteurs spécialisés.

Groupes limités.

Grand domaine avec terrains multiples, rivière pour canoë-kayak ; piscine olympique.

Hébergement de qualité dans maisonnettes ou chambres.

Cuisine simple mais très soignée.

Prix : 4 000 francs tout compris *(sauf équipements sportifs individuels loués sur place).*

Inscriptions avant le 15 juin

The Four Winds Club

Summer course, from 1 - 15 July

Place : Lozère.

The countryside and a great many possibilities for sport : rock climbing, water sports, cycling, horse riding, tennis, team sports, etc... all under the supervision of specialised instructors.

Small groups.

Extensive grounds with numerous sports fields, a river for canoeing, olympic-sized swimming pool.

Excellent accommodation in individual cottages or rooms.

Simple, well-prepared food.

Price : 4,000 francs all inclusive (except individual sports equipment rented locally).

Enrolments before 15 June.

Sports

38

There are major sporting events throughout the year in France : in June, the international tennis championships at Roland-Garros ; in July, the Tour de France ; in the autumn, the "Course du Rhum" (solo transatlantic sailing race) ; in the Spring, the "24 heures du Mans" (motor racing), the "Bol d'or" and "le Castelet" (motorcycles).

As elsewhere, the major national and international football and rugby championships have a major following in France.

It is easier to do sport in the provinces than in Paris (owing to available space and the corresponding price of using the facilities).

In Paris, on the other hand, there are many keep-fit clubs and gymnasiums.

VOCABULARY

un stade	stadium
un arbitre	referee, umpire
une équipe	team
une balle	ball (tennis,...)
un ballon	ball (football, ...)
une bicyclette	bicycle
l'alpinisme	montaineering
le football	soccer
un filet	net
une raquette	racket
la gymnastique	gymnastics
la natation	swimming
le ski	skiing, ski
la voile	sailing, sail
le volley-ball	volleyball
un sportif	athletic person
un club	club
une compétition	competition
une épreuve	event
courir	to run
gagner	to win
jouer	to play
nager	to swim
perdre	to lose
pratiquer	to practise, play
s'inscrire	to join, enrol

GRAMMAR

Prepositions :

à (at, in, to), **avant** (before), **avec** (with), **chez** (at someone's house, among), **dans** (in, inside), **de** (from, of), **derrière** (behind), **devant** (in front of), **en** (in, by), **par** (by, through), **pendant** (for, during), **pour** (for, in order to), **sous** (under), **sur** (on), **vers** (towards, about).
Prepositions are followed by a noun or pronoun.
J'aimerais m'inscrire à l'association.

The recent past : «venir de» + the infinitive

The recent past refers to an action that has just been completed.
Mon équipe vient de gagner un match.

EXERCISES

1. Choose the appropriate preposition.

de - dans - avec - à - pour

Je m'entraîne ... la piscine ... mon frère.
Il fait ... l'équitation ... un très bon club.
... jouer, il faut une carte ... membre.

2. Transform the following sentences using the recent past.

Il fait de l'escalade → Il vient de faire de l'escalade.

Nous jouons au football.
Vous gagnez une nouvelle médaille.
Tu cours beaucoup.
Je me suis inscrite au club sportif.

3. Translate.

J'aimerais faire plus de marche. On a regardé le match à la télé chez mes amis. Pendant la journée on peut s'entraîner derrière le stade.

KEY TO EXERCISES

1. à / avec - de / dans - pour / de
2. Nous venons de jouer. Vous venez de gagner. Tu viens de courir beaucoup. Je viens de m'inscrire.
3. I would like to do more walking. We watched the match on TV at my friends' house. During the day, we can train behind the stadium.

HOW TO SAY IT !

Ce qu'on peut faire (la possibilité) :

– Tu peux/on peut choisir...
– Tu as/on a le droit d'aller à la piscine.
– On a (tu as...) le choix entre... et ...
– Il est possible de...

What you can do (possibility) :

– You/one can choose ...
– You/one are/is allowed to go to the swimming pool
– One (you) have the choice between... and...
– It is possible to...

Ce qu'on préfère :

– Je préfère...
– J'aime mieux le football/ce moniteur.
– J'aimerais mieux...
– Je préfèrerais faire du tennis.

What you prefer :

– I prefer...
– I prefer football / this instructor.
– I'd rather...
– I'd rather play tennis.

I feel really great !
(Lit. : "I have a peach from hell")

Le répondeur : Bonjour ! Vous êtes bien au 46 62 10 55. Nous ne sommes pas là pour le moment. Mais laissez-nous votre nom et votre numéro de téléphone après le signal sonore et nous vous rappellerons dès notre retour. À bientôt !

– C'est Emmanuel, je téléphonais pour confirmer le rendez-vous de samedi. Je serai à la maison ce soir. J'attends votre coup de fil.

– C'est Sophie. Je t'appelle parce que je ne peux pas venir demain. Je m'en vais en week-end avec mes parents. Désolée. Je te rappelle plus tard. Je t'embrasse.

The answering machine : Hello ! This is 46.62.10.55. We are not in at the moment, but leave us your name and telephone number after the beep and we'll call you as soon as we return. Speak to you later !

– Emmanuel speaking. I'm calling to confirm our rendez-vous on Saturday. I'll be at home this evening. I'll look forward to your call. 'Bye !

– It's Sophie. I'm calling because I can't make it tomorrow. I'm going away with my parents for the week-end. Sorry. I'll call you later. See you.

BON À SAVOIR

In 1990, 95 % of French households had at least one telephone compared with just 22.8 % in 1973 and almost one in five subscribers possessed a "Minitel" - a small computer terminal giving access to the electronic telephone directory (dial 11) and a host of other services (dial 36 15...) such as making reservations, getting weather forecasts or Stock Market prices, playing games and even communicating with other subscribers ...

French telephone numbers (8 digits) are divided into 2 zones : Paris and the rest of France. The 8-digit numbers are used within each zone but calls between Paris and the provinces and vice-versa require the following additions : Paris → Provinces : 16 + 8 digits, Provinces → Paris : 16.1 + 8 digits.

When making an international call from France, dial 19, wait for the tone and then dial the country dialling code, area code + subscriber's number.

VOCABULARY

un annuaire	(telephone) directory
un appareil	telephone
un répondeur	answering machine
une cabine	telephone box
un combiné	receiver
un dérangement	out of order
une erreur	mistake
une facture	bill, invoice
un indicatif	dialling code
une ligne	line
une message	message
les réclamations	complaints
les renseignements	inquiries
une sonnerie	ringing, bell
une télécarte	'phone card
occupé	engaged
appeler	to call
composer	to dial
décrocher	to lift the receiver
parler	to speak
répondre	to answer
se tromper	to dial the wrong number
téléphoner	to phone

GRAMMAR

The future :

The future is formed from the stem of the verb + **«-rai, -ras, -ra, -rons, -rez, -ront»**

Tu téléphoneras. - Elle parlera.

Vous :

«Vous» is used when speaking to several people (plural) or as a polite form (without the intimacy of **«tu»**) when addressing a stranger, or someone your senior (age, hierarchy, etc.).

EXERCISES

1. Put into the future.

Tu m'appelles vers 20 heures ? → Tu m'appelleras vers 20 heures ?

Le téléphone sonne souvent. Nous décrochons dès que nous entendons le téléphone. Je laisse un message sur ton répondeur. Vous écoutez la conversation.

2. Put the following sentences into the present indicative.

Vous *(décrocher)* le combiné, puis vous *(introduire)* votre carte. Les enfants ! Vous *(arrêter)* de jouer avec le téléphone ? Lors de votre voyage, vous *(pouvoir)* aussi me téléphoner en P.C.V.

3. Fill in the gaps in the following conversation.

« ... . Est-ce que je pourrais parler à Pierre ?
– Non, il ..... là. C'est de la part de ..... ?
– C'est Marie. Vous ..... lui dire que j'ai ..... . J'aimerais qu'il me ..... à son retour.
– D'accord, je n'y manquerai pas. Au revoir.
– ..... »

KEY TO EXERCISES

1. sonnera - décrocherons / entendrons - laisserai - écouterez.
2. décrochez / introduisez - arrêtez - pouvez.
3. Bonjour - n'est pas / qui - pouvez / appelé (téléphoné) / téléphone (rappelle) (n° de téléphone) - Merci. Au revoir.

HOW TO SAY IT !

POUR TÉLÉPHONER :

– Allô ?
– Bonjour !
– Est-ce que .... est là ?
– Est-ce que je pourrais parler à mademoiselle/madame/monsieur ... ?
– Vous vous trompez. – Vous faites erreur. – Quel numéro demandez-vous ?
– Excusez-moi je me suis trompé(e) de numéro.
– Ne quittez pas, nous recherchons votre correspondant.
– Bonjour ! Pierre Leduc, s'il vous plaît !

USING THE TELEPHONE :

– Hello
– Hello
– Is ... there ?
– Could I speak to Miss / Mrs / Mr ... ?
– You've got the wrong number.
– You've made a mistake.
– What number do you want ?
– I'm sorry, I dialled the wrong number.
– Hold the line. We're trying to connect you.
– Hello ! Pierre Leduc, please !

I can't hear very well. There's crackle on the line.
(friture = fried food/crackle)

Télévision

– J'ai regardé le journal télévisé de 20 heures hier sur la Cinq. Il y a eu d'excellents reportages.
– Moi, je préfère écouter la radio, surtout les informations. Des fois je les écoute à 7 heures sur Europe 1, après il y a la revue de presse à 8 h et demie. Et bien sûr, les infos de 13 heures sur France-Inter !
– Et tu regardes quoi comme émissions à la télé ?
– Un peu de tout. J'ai le Câble. Alors je reçois une vingtaine de chaînes dans toutes les langues. On est aussi abonné à Canal plus.
– Tu lis des journaux aussi ?
– Oui, un hebdo, de temps en temps, mais on finit quand même par se retrouver devant la télé.

– I watched the news at 8 o'clock on La Cinq yesterday. There were some excellent reports.
– I prefer listening to the radio, especially the news. Sometimes I listen to it at 7 o'clock in the morning on Europe 1 followed by the review of the press at half past eight. And, of course, the 1 p.m. news on France-Inter !
– And what programmes do you watch on the telly ?
– A bit of everything. I've got cable TV. So I receive about twenty channels in different languages. We've also got Canal Plus*.
– Do you read newspapers too ?
– Yes, a weekly from time to time, but we still end up in front of the telly !

*Canal Plus is a private encrypted channel.

• 95% of French people possess at least one TV set. Seven channels broadcast nationwide (**TF1**, Antenne 2, **FR3**, Canal Plus, La Cinq, M6, La Sept) in addition to local channels. Antenne 2 and **FR3** are state-controlled; the others belong to the private sector.
Paris and several other large towns (Orléans, Rennes, Rouen...) are linked to the cable TV network (for which subscribers are charged) enabling viewers to obtain European and American channels.
• A wide range of stations can be obtained on the radio:
Of the so-called "peripheral stations" ("les périphériques" whose transmitter is situated outside France), the most popular are RTL (Radio Télé Luxembourg), Europe 1 and RMC (Radio Monte-Carlo).
• There is also a wide variety of "theme" radio stations broadcasting on the FM band ("modulation de fréquence": frequency modulation) in addition to all the radio stations belonging to Radio-France (public sector).

VOCABULARY

un(e) journaliste	journalist
un(e) présentateur(trice)	introducer, presenter
une antenne	aerial
le câble	cable TV
une caméra	camera
une cassette	cassette
un magnétoscope	video cassette recorder
un micro(phone)	microphone
une station	station
la vidéo	video
une chaîne	channel
une émission	programme, broadcast
les infos	news
un journal	(TV) journal
les média(s)	the media
un programme	programme
un reportage	report
une revue de presse	press review
quotidien	a daily (newspaper)
privé	private
enregistrer	to record

GRAMMAR

■ *The present indicative of Group 2 verbs :*

They are conjugated in the same way as **«finir»**

je finis	*nous finissons*
tu finis	*vous finissez*
il finit	*ils finissent*

▲ Do not confuse with other verbs ending in **«-ir»** which belong to Group 3. (See the Grammar Summary.)

EXERCISES

1. Choose the appropriate word.

chaînes – émission – journaux – présentateur

As-tu vu cette ..... ?
Ce ..... est très célèbre.
Nous recevons seulement trois ..... .
Je lis beaucoup de ..... .

2. Choose the correct form of the verb* «finir» *in the present tense.

Tu ..... quand ?
Vous ..... ce travail maintenant ?
On ..... par comprendre en réfléchissant.
Je ne ..... pas cet article, il m'ennuie

3. Put into the perfect tense.

Je sors une cassette. → J'ai sorti une cassette.

Nous partons trop tard.
On choisit quelle émission ?
Je dors devant la télé.
Ils établissent les programmes.

KEY TO EXERCISES

1. émission – présentateur – chaînes – journaux.
2. finis – finissez – finit – finis.
3. sommes parti(e)s – a choisi – j'ai dormi – ont établi.

HOW TO SAY IT !

Comment exprimer

• ses préférences :

– J'aime bien les émissions sportives.
– Je préfère les magazines d'actualité.
– J'adore les feuilletons, surtout américains.

• un jugement négatif :

– L'été, il n'y a rien à la télé !

– C'est de plus en plus inintéressant.
– Qu'est-ce que c'est mauvais !
– C'est toujours la même chose !

Expressing

• preference :

– I like sports programmes.

– I prefer current affairs programmes.
– I love serials, especially American ones.

• a negative opinion :

– In summer, there's nothing on the telly!
– It's getting more and more uninteresting.
– It's really bad!
– It's always the same thing!

Couldn't we have a different channel ?
(chaîne = chain/TV channel)

Info n° 8

A.-P. Neyrat / Rapho

Marché aux Puces

If you want to renew your wardrobe, go window shopping in the rue Montaigne or place des Victoires where the leading fashion designers ("grands couturiers") have set up shop. You will find their clothes and other, less expensive models, in the large Parisian department stores : Le Bon Marché (rue de Sèvres), La Samaritaine (rue de Rivoli), Le Printemps and Galeries La Fayette (near Gare Saint-Lazare).

There are two large shopping centres in Paris : Montparnasse and the Forum des Halles.

• If your finances are somewhat limited, try Tati (rue de Rennes, boulevard Barbès, place de la République) or go for a stroll on a Sunday morning around the secondhand clothes stalls and antiques in the Puces (flea market) (porte de Clignancourt, porte de Montreuil).

• The department stores and a great many shops offer tax refunds ("détaxe") for foreign visitors or non-residents. The actual refund takes place when you leave France (you give the relevant papers to the "Détaxe" office at the port or airport), so allow plenty of extra time!

• The avenue de l'Opéra has a great many shops for tourists - so-called *"Free taxe"* shops selling luxury items, leather goods, perfume...

Souvenirs can be found under the arcades of the rue de Rivoli just a few minutes walk away...

Don't forget the Latin Quarter for books, especially the boulevard Saint-Michel and boulevard Saint-Germain...

– Pour aller en Bretagne en voiture, à partir de Paris, vous pouvez prendre l'autoroute de l'Ouest. Mais si vous avez le temps, préférez les itinéraires verts (bis) et les petites routes de campagne qui ont beaucoup de charme. Il vous faudra seulement bien étudier la carte et, en chemin, faites attention aux panneaux indiquant les routes départementales ou les nationales, plus importantes. À vous de voir.
– Et si nous voulons visiter la petite ville dont vous parliez ?
– Renseignez-vous au syndicat d'initiative ou à l'office du tourisme. Ils sauront vous conseiller sur tout ce qu'il faut voir dans la région !

– To go to Brittany from Paris by car, you can take the West motorway. But if you have the time, take the secondary, scenic routes and the small country roads that are very charming. You will simply have to study the map and, as you drive along, watch out for the road signs indicating the B roads or the more important A roads. It's up to you to decide.
– And if we want to visit that small town you were talking about ?
– Inquire at the information bureau or tourist office ! They'll be able to advise you about what you should see in the region !

Although many French people prefer to travel by car, the National French Railways, or **S.N.C.F.** *("Société nationale des chemins de fer"), attracts many travellers impressed by the punctuality of the trains!*
Air Inter, the main carrier on domestic air routes, is facing growing competition from the new high-speed **T.G.V.** *("train à grande vitesse"). If you intend to travel by* **T.G.V**, *remember to book a seat beforehand (this is compulsory). You can do this by 'phone, Minitel (code:* **S.N.C.F.**) *or at the station itself.*
For details about places of interest in each region and province, consult one of the many guidebooks available - "Le Guide Bleu" (Hachette), "Les Guides Verts" (Michelin) on the different regions, "Le Guide du Routard" among others...

VOCABULARY

un touriste	tourist
un office de tourisme	tourist information office
un aéroport	airport
un avion	aeroplane
une carte	map
un dépliant	leaflet
un plan	map, plan
un guide	guide
un itinéraire	itinerary
une gare	station
un quai (de gare)	(station) platform
un train	train
une voiture (de train)	(railway) carriage
la campagne	country(side)
un département	French administrative region
une île	island
la/une province	province
un village	village
détaillé	detailed
la distance	distance
pittoresque	picturesque
(se) renseigner	to make inquiries
visiter	to visit

GRAMMAR

▮ *The infinitive:*

A verb is in the infinitive :

- **when it follows another verb:**
  Tu vas traverser l'Alsace. Nous voulons visiter Rouen.
- **after a preposition:**
  Pour aller là-bas... Réserve avant de partir.

▮ *The verb* savoir *in the present indicative :*

je sais - tu sais - il sait - nous savons - vous savez - ils savent.

In the future: Je saurai... - **in the perfect tense:** J'ai su...

In the imperfect: je savais...

EXERCISES

1. Put into the immediate future.

Tu choisiras cet itinéraire. → Tu vas choisir cet itinéraire.

Il suivra la nationale.
Elle traversera la Manche.
Nous verrons les touristes.

2. Join the sentences together using an infinitive.

Réservez vos places. C'est nécessaire.
Tourne à droite. Regarde le plan avant.
Visitons l'église. Nous le pouvons.

3. Translate.

Je ne sais pas comment y aller. On a pris le T.G.V. pour aller à Brest. La campagne est belle par ici.

KEY TO EXERCISES

1. Il va suivre. - Elle va traverser. - Nous allons voir.
2. C'est nécessaire de réserver vos places. - Regarde le plan avant de tourner. - Nous pouvons visiter l'église.
3. I don't know how to go there. We took the T.G.V. to go to Brest. The countryside is beautiful around here.

HOW TO SAY IT !

CHOISIR/PARLER D'UN MOYEN DE TRANSPORT :

– On y va en train ou en voiture ?
– Tu prends le bateau ou l'avion ?

CHOOSING/TALKING ABOUT A MEANS OF TRANSPORT :

– Shall we go by train or by car ?
– Are you taking the boat or the 'plane ?

FORMULER UN CHOIX, UNE PRÉFÉRENCE :

– Si vous préférez, allez-y en vélo !
– J'aimerais autant un petit hôtel.
– Qu'est-ce que tu préfères ?
– On choisit quoi ?
– Et si on prenait le car ?

EXPRESSING A CHOICE, A PREFERENCE :

– If you'd rather, go there on bicycle.
– I'd just as well (stay in) a small hotel.
– What do you prefer ?
– What shall we choose ?
– And what if we took the coach ?

Let's get off the beaten track.

– Bonjour, monsieur.
– Bonjour.
– Je voudrais aller à la tour Eiffel, mais je ne sais pas comment...
– Vous avez plusieurs solutions : le métro, le RER ou l'autobus. Mais dans tous les cas, vous allez devoir marcher un peu.
– Oh ! Pas de problème, j'aime la marche.
– Bon, alors vous pouvez prendre le 72 et descendre à Trocadéro. Vous aurez à traverser le pont d'léna. Avec le bus vous profiterez de la vue. Si vous êtes pressé, prenez le métro, c'est plus rapide ; vous descendez à la station Bir-Hakeim.
– Bien. Je crois que je vais prendre le bus. Merci.

– Hello.
– Hello.
– I'd like to go to the Eiffel Tower, but I don't know how ...
– You have several solutions : the metro, the RER or the bus. But either way, you will have to walk a little.
– Oh, that's no problem. I like walking.
– Well then, you can take the n° 72 bus and get off at Trocadéro. You'll have to cross the pont d'léna. With the bus, you'll enjoy the view. If you're in a hurry, take the metro, it's faster. Get off at the Bir-Hakeim station.
– Well. I think I'll take the bus. Thanks.

Transport

The Paris "Métropolitain" or "métro" (underground) was built at the end of the **19th** *century by Fulgence Bienvenüe and covers Paris and its immediate suburbs. It runs nearly all day, from 5 a.m. until 1 a.m.*
A new express service (the **"R.E.R."** *for "Réseau express régional") now provides fast links between Paris and the suburbs on 4 lines : A, B, C and D. The* **RATP** *("Régie autonome des transports parisiens" - the Paris Transport Authority) has the monopoly of all public transport ("transports en commun") in Paris (bus, metro).*
Some other large cities, such as Lille, Lyon, Marseille and shortly Toulouse and Rouen, boast their own métro. Automatic systems (i.e. trains without drivers, such as the **"VAL"** *system in Lille) are becoming more common. Some towns still have tramways (Saint-Etienne, Nantes, Grenoble...).*
Don't forget to ask about special rates for tourists (cheap day passes...).

VOCABULARY

un arrêt (d'autobus)	(bus) stop
une correspondance	connection
un billet	ticket
un carnet	book of tickets
une carte orange	season ticket
un forfait	set price
un guichet	ticket office
un horaire	timetable
un itinéraire	itinerary
une ligne	line
un plan	(street) map, plan
un train	train
un chauffeur	driver
un conducteur	(engine) driver
un contrôleur	(ticket) inspector
(s')arrêter	to stop
changer (de bus, de métro)	to change (buses, underground trains)
descendre	to get off
faire signe	to make a sign
longer	to border, to go along
monter	to get on
payer	to pay

GRAMMAR

The immediate future

The immediate future is used to express an imminent action.

It is formed by using the verb "aller" in the present indicative followed by the main verb in the infinitive :

Je vais prendre le bus. Vous allez devoir marcher.

EXERCISES

1. *Put into the immediate future.*

Ma femme part en vacances après-demain. → Ma femme va partir en vacances après-demain.

Paul et Luc prennent le R.E.R.
Nous travaillons à la R.A.T.P.
Tu connais la S.N.C.F. ?
C'est la fête du village. Tu y assistes ?

2. *Put the verbs in brackets into the future or immediate future.*

L'année prochaine je *(s'inscrire)* à la fac des sciences.
Le métro *(arriver)* dans quelques minutes.
Quand *(avoir)* de l'argent je *(acheter)* une voiture.
Tu *(ne pas prendre)* l'autobus à cette heure-ci !
Attention, ne montez plus : le train *(partir).*

3. *True or false ? (See the "Bon à savoir" section.)*

Le R.E.R. est un train lent.
Le métro date du XIXe siècle.
Le métro parisien roule 24 heures sur 24.
Il y a un tramway à Nantes.

KEY TO EXERCISES

1. Paul et Luc vont prendre... - Nous allons travailler... - Tu vas connaître... - Tu vas y assister...
2. m'inscrirai - va arriver - j'aurai/j'achèterai - Tu ne vas pas prendre... - va partir.
3. false - true - false - true.

HOW TO SAY IT !

Demander un conseil :

– Pouvez-vous me dire où est l'arrêt du bus ?
– Savez-vous où est la station de métro ?
– Connaissez-vous la ligne A ?

Asking for advice :

– Can you tell me where the bus stop is ?
– Do you know where the metro station is ?
– Do you know line A ?

Donner un conseil :

– Prenez/prends l'autobus.
– Le mieux, c'est de changer à Châtelet.
– Je vous conseille de prendre le R.E.R.
– Vous pouvez prendre un taxi.
– Ne prenez pas le métro ou le bus aux heures de pointe.

Giving advice :

– Take the bus.
– The best thing is to change at Châtelet.
– I advise you to take the R.E.R.
– You can take a taxi.
– Don't take the metro or the bus during the rush hours.

We're packed in like sardines.

– Alors Loïc, toujours à la recherche d'un travail ?
– Et non, je ne suis plus au chômage depuis hier.
– Ça c'est super ! Qu'est-ce que tu as trouvé ?
– Un poste à mi-temps dans une boîte d'informatique, tu sais que j'ai suivi un stage grâce à l'A.N.P.E.[1]. On m'a demandé : « Ça vous plairait de faire de l'informatique ? » Je croyais que je n'y arriverais pas et puis ça a très bien marché.
– Tu voudrais continuer des stages tout en travaillant ?
– Oui, mon nouveau patron me l'a déjà dit : « Avec une bonne formation en mathématiques, vous feriez un excellent informaticien. »

– Well then, Loïc, still looking for a job ?
– No, I stopped being unemployed yesterday.
– That's great ! What did you find ?
– A half-time job in a computer company. You know that I attended a training course through the A.N.P.E. (1). They asked me : "Would you like to do computing ?" I thought I wouldn't manage to do it but it worked very well.
– Would you like to continue training while you work ?
– Yes, my new boss has already told me : "With good training in mathematics, you'd make an excellent computer technician."

---

(1) "Agence nationale pour l'emploi" or National Employment Agency.

BON À SAVOIR

French employees work a 39-hour week and enjoy 5 weeks paid holiday. In **1990**, 2.5 million people were registered as unemployed.

All employees pay contributions ("cotisations ") to the social security ("la sécurité sociale" or "sécu") and a pension fund ("une caisse de retraite"). There is an official minimum salary known as the **S.M.I.C.** (for "salaire minimum interprofessionnel de croissance").
Job-seekers receive unemployment benefits ("indemnités") for a limited period and when this comes to an end, they can receive the **R.M.I.** ("revenu minimum d'insertion professionnelle") available to anyone without financial resources. The right to go on strike is guaranteed by the French Constitution and the 1st of May ("La fête du travail" - labour day) is a national bank holiday.

VOCABULARY

un emploi	job, employment
un job	temporary job
un métier	trade
un syndicat	union
un artisan	craftsman
un artiste	artist
un chômeur	unemployed person
un commerçant	shopkeeper
un directeur	manager
un employé	employee, clerk
un ingénieur	engineer
une secrétaire	secretary
un spécialiste	specialist
une administration	administration
un bureau	office
une usine	factory
les congés	holidays
un curriculum vitae	curriculum vitae
une grève	strike
une rémunération	remuneration
la retraite	retirement
un salaire	salary
bosser (fam.)	to work (colloquial)
travailler	to work

GRAMMAR

■ *The conditional :*

The conditional is formed using the stem of the verb used to form the future + the endings of the imperfect tense : **-ais, -ais, -ait, -ions, -iez, -aient.**

J'aimerais travailler. Vous pourriez vous former.

The conditional is used to express a wish, a request or a condition: **Si** + the imperfect + the present conditional.

S'il n'était pas au chômage, il gagnerait de l'argent.

EXERCISES

1. Put into the conditional :

Je gagne certainement beaucoup dans cette entreprise. → Je gagnerais certainement beaucoup dans cette entreprise.

Elle souhaite travailler avec des enfants.
Je peux trouver un travail pour l'été.
Tu aimes travailler ici ?

2. Put into the appropriate tense :

Si on les *(payer)* mieux, ils ne *(faire)* pas grève.
Si tu *(être)* vétérinaire, tu t'*(occuper)* d'animaux.
Si je *(pouvoir)* faire des études, j'*(aimer)* être publicitaire.

3. Translate :

Il est à la retraite depuis un an.
J'ai suivi un stage pour me spécialiser en programmation.
Ils font grève pour demander une augmentation de salaire.
Elle a perdu son emploi et se trouve au chômage.

KEY TO EXERCISES

1. souhaiterait - pourrais - aimerais.
2. payait/feraient - étais/occuperais - pouvais/aimerais.
3. He's been retired for a year. I attended a training course to become specialised in programming. They are on strike (to ask) for an increase in salary. She has lost her job and finds herself unemployed.

HOW TO SAY IT !

POUR EXPRIMER UN SOUHAIT, UN DÉSIR :

– J'aimerais m'occuper d'adolescents.
– Je voudrais faire de l'informatique.
– Ça me plairait de faire de la recherche.
– Si je pouvais, j'aimerais être médecin.

EXPRESSING A WISH OR A DESIRE :

– I'd like to look after teenagers.
– I'd like to work in computing.
– I'd like to do research.
– If I could, I'd like to be a doctor.

POUR DIRE SON IGNORANCE :

– Je ne sais pas du tout quel métier choisir.
– Quelle profession exercer ?
– Je n'en sais rien ! Aucune idée ! Alors là !

EXPRESSING ONE'S IGNORANCE:

– I don't know at all what job to choose.
– What profession could I (you, he, etc...) do ?
– I don't know ! No idea ! It beats me !

You work too much !
(bosse = hump ; bosser = to work)

Vacances

– Où allez-vous en vacances cet été ?

– En Bretagne. Nous avons loué une grande maison près de la mer. Mon mari veut faire de la planche à voile. Moi, j'ai horreur de ça, je suis épuisée au bout de cinq minutes, je préfère me reposer et me promener sur la plage. Et toi, où vas-tu ?

– Dans le Jura, comme l'été dernier. Nous y sommes déjà allés cet hiver pour faire du ski ; j'y retourne pour faire des randonnées avec des amis. Il y a moins de monde sur les sentiers de montagne que sur les plages !

– Where are you going on holiday this summer ?

– To Brittany. We have rented a large house near the sea. My husband wants to go wind-surfing. Personally, I hate it. I'm exhausted after five minutes. I prefer to relax and walk on the beach. And where are you going ?

– To the Jura, as we did last summer. We went there skiing this winter. I'm going back there to go hiking with friends. There are fewer people on mountain paths than on the beaches !

BON À SAVOIR

The main holiday periods coincide with the school holidays ("congés scolaires"): Christmas, Easter and the long summer holidays ("les grandes vacances")
All employees have the right to take (under certain conditions) five weeks paid leave every year.
More than **50 %** *of French people go away for their summer holidays and many people go skiing at Christmas, in February ("vacances de neige" for school children) or at Easter in the Alps or Pyrenees.*
If you want to enjoy the peace and quiet of the countryside, go walking in France along the paths specially marked for hikers ("sentiers de Grande Randonnée" or **G.R.**).
The "Institut géographique national" (**I.G.N.**) *produces detailed maps of these paths.*

VOCABULARY

l'alpinisme	mountainering
une balade	stroll
l'escalade	(rock) climbing
la voile	sailing
un moniteur	instructor
la sieste	siesta, snooze
un coup de soleil	sunstroke
une dune	dune
un maillot de bain	swimming costume
la marée	tide
la neige	snow
une piste	track, (ski) run
le sable	sand
un chalet	chalet
un guide	guide
un refuge	refuge, mountain hut
une station	resort
un téléphérique	cable-car
un sac à dos	rucksack
(se) baigner	to bath
bronzer	to get a tan
marcher	to walk, hike
nager	to swim
skier	to ski

GRAMMAR

■ *Two irregular verbs :*

- **In the present indicative :**

1. Aller	2. Faire
Je vais	*Je fais*
Tu vas	*Tu fais*
Il va	*Il fait*
Nous allons	*Nous faisons*
Vous allez	*Vous faites*
Ils vont	*Ils font*

- **The future :**
  1. *J'irai - tu iras - il ira - nous irons - vous irez - ils iront.*
  2. *Je ferai - tu feras - il fera - nous ferons - vous ferez - ils feront.*
- **The perfect tense :**
  1. *je suis allé(e) - tu es allé(e)...*
  2. *j'ai fait - tu as fait...*

EXERCISES

1. *Choose the appropriate word.*

voile - piste - station - baigner.

Si tu skies bien, prends la ..... noire. J'aime bien me ..... le matin. Ils adorent la mer, ils font de la ..... . Il y a beaucoup de monde dans cette .....

2. *Choose the correct form of the verb "aller" in the appropriate tense.*

Je ne ..... jamais au cinéma en été. Ils ..... souvent au marché. Est-ce que tu ..... à la montagne le mois prochain ? On ..... à la plage hier.

3. *Put into the appropriate tense (future or perfect).*

Tu fais de la voile, et hier ? → J'ai fait de la voile aussi.

Tu fais du vélo, et demain ? Vous faites du ski, et demain ? Vous faites des affaires, et hier ? Tu fais du yoga, et hier ?

KEY TO EXERCISES

1. piste - baigner - voile - station.
2. vais - vont - iras - est allé.
3. je ferai - Nous ferons - Nous avons fait - J'ai fait.

HOW TO SAY IT !

POUR RACONTER

• CE QU'ON A FAIT :

– L'été dernier, j'ai fait toute l'Italie.
– On a pris/nous avons pris la voiture.
– On y est allé en train/en avion.
– On a découvert une belle région.

• CE QU'ON VA FAIRE :

– L'année prochaine, on fait le tour du monde.
– Nous irons voir la famille.

– J'aimerais visiter l'Andalousie.

SAYING

• WHAT YOU HAVE DONE :

– Last summer, I did all of Italy...
– We took the car...

– We went by train/'plane...

– We discovered a beautiful region.

• WHAT YOU ARE GOING TO DO :

– Next year, we're going around the world.
– We're going to see our relations.
– I'd like to visit Andalusia.

Ah ! To be able to relax !
(doigts de pied en éventail = splayed toes/toes like a fan)

Exceptionnel !

Notre nouveau modèle vient d'arriver !

Souple et nerveuse. Une ligne superbe. Un moteur six cylindres. Quatre roues motrices. Un système de freinage ABS. Une tenue de route parfaite, grâce à son ordinateur de bord.

Des sièges confortables et réglables. Un coffre vaste pour vos bagages. Des vitres teintées à ouverture électrique. Une carrosserie bien protégée (peinture anti-corrosion).

Sur ce modèle haut de gamme, vous aurez des phares anti-brouillard de série, et naturellement, vous pourrez utiliser l'essence sans plomb.

Venez l'essayer sans engagement de votre part !

EXCEPTIONAL !

Our new model has just arrived !

Flexible with good acceleration. Superb lines. A six-cylinder engine. Four-wheel drive. An ABS braking system. Perfect road-holding thanks to its on-board computer.

Comfortable, adjustable seats. An immense boot for your luggage. Tinted, electric windows. Fully protected bodywork (anti-rust paint).

On this up-market model, fog lights are fitted as standard and, naturally, you can use lead-free petrol.

Come for a test drive, without obligation on your part !

Eighteen is the minimum age for holding a licence to drive a car (although it is possible to drive as a learner as early as 16 when accompanied by an adult). Insurance ("assurance") is compulsory for all motor vehicles.

The main French motor manufacturers are Peugeot, Citroën and Renault.

Cars are sold via a network of dealers representing a particular marque. They are responsible for supplying spare parts ("pièces détachées"), providing services under guarantee, etc.

An annual motor show ("Mondial de l'automobile") presents new models to the public.

VOCABULARY

une auto(mobile)	motorcar
une batterie	battery
le capot	bonnet
la ceinture de sécurité	safety belt
les freins	brakes
un clignotant	indicator
un essuie-glace	windscreen wiper
un pare-brise	windscreen
un pare-chocs	bumpers
un phare	headlight
un pneu	tyre
une portière	door
un rétroviseur	rear-view mirror
une roue (de secours)	spare wheel
le volant	steering wheel
une assurance	insurance
un bidon	can
la consommation	consumption
le gasoil	diesel
l'huile	oil
un permis (de conduire)	(driving) licence
un(e) conducteur(trice)	driver
un passager	passenger
faire le plein	to fill up (with petrol)

GRAMMAR

▮ *Demonstrative adjectives :*

ce + a masculine singular noun.
cette + a feminine singular noun : *Cette voiture*
ces + a plural noun (masculine or feminine) : *Ces moteurs*
▲ **cet** + a masculine singular noun beginning with a vowel or silent "h" : *Cet arbre. Cet hiver. Cet homme.*

▮ *Demonstrative pronouns :*

celui (masculine singular) : *Ce vélo est celui de mon frère.*
celle (feminine singular) : *Cette voiture est celle de ma mère.*
ceux (masculine plural) : *Ces pneus sont ceux que tu vends.*
celles (feminine plural) : *Ces annonces sont celles qui m'intéressent.*
▲ **ce/c'/ceci/cela** (neutral demonstrative pronouns) :
Il faut acheter une voiture, cela est nécessaire. Écoute ceci !
▲ In the spoken (as opposed to written) language, **"ça"** is often used instead of **"cela"**.

EXERCISES

1. Choose the appropriate word :

sièges – essence – coffre – pneus

Achète de l'..... sans plomb. J'ai des ..... neufs. Les ..... sont très confortables. Mets la valise dans le ..... !

2. Transform the following sentences as shown in the example :

Achète ce vélo. → Achète celui-ci.
Change cette roue. → Change celle-ci.

Vérifie cette batterie. Enlève ce pneu. Essaie ces lunettes de soleil. Vends ces moteurs.

3. Use the appropriate demonstrative pronoun :

Cette batterie est ... que je viens d'acheter. À qui est ce permis ? C'est ..... de mon père. Ces assurances sont bien ..... que nous avons. ..... vous intéresse ?

KEY TO EXERCISES

1. essence – pneus – sièges – coffre.
2. celle-ci – celui-ci – celles-ci – ceux-ci.
3. celle – celui – celles – cela / ça.

HOW TO SAY IT !

Comment rédiger une petite annonce (pour vendre une voiture) :

**Vends Peugeot 205 rouge – modèle 1985 – première main – 80 000 km – pneus neufs – entretien régulier – carrosserie impeccable.
Prix argus : 25 000 francs.**

How to write a classified ad (to sell a car) :

*For sale (lit. "I sell") : red Peugeot 205 - 1985 model - first hand - 80,000 km - new tyres - serviced regularly - perfect bodywork. Argus * price : 25,000 francs.*

*"*L'Argus*", a weekly magazine of classified ads for second-hand vehicles, gives lists of standard trade-in prices for second-hand vehicles per model and per year.

Look at that car !
(caisse = crate/car)

Grammar

Nouns

Plural of nouns 208

Articles

Definite article 208
Indefinite article 209
Partitive article 209
Omission of the definite article 209

Adjectives

Demonstrative adjectives 210
Possessive adjectives 210
Cardinal numbers 211
Fractions 212
Decimals 212
Percentages 212
Adjectives of quality 212

Comparative of adjectives

Comparative of superiority 214
Comparative of inferiority 214
Comparative of equality 214

summary

Superlative of adjectives
Superlative relative 214
Superlative absolute 215

Pronouns
Personal pronouns 215
Demonstrative pronouns 217
Possessive pronouns 217
Relative pronouns 218

Adverbs
Formation of adverbs
ending in « -ment » 219
Position of adverbs in the sentence 220

Verbs
Conjugations 220
Tenses and moods 220
Verb tables 223

NOUNS

The formation of plurals

Most nouns form their plural by adding an *s* to the singular.
Un enfant → des enfants.

• Nouns already ending in *-s, -z* or *-x* in the singular remain unchanged in the plural:
un fils → des fils   *un gaz → des gaz*   *une voix → des voix*

• Most nouns ending in *-au, -eau, -eu* in the singular, add an *x* in the plural:
un bateau → des bateaux   *un cheveu → des cheveux*

▲ Words ending in *-al* change to *-aux*:
Un journal → des journaux

ARTICLES

The definite article

The definite article is used when referring to particular persons or things, which have already been mentioned. It is also used when the noun is used in a general sense, referring to abstractions or to all things of a kind.

<table>
<tr><th></th><th>singular</th><th>plural</th></tr>
<tr><td>masculine</td><td>le garçon</td><td rowspan="3">les enfants</td></tr>
<tr><td rowspan="1">masculine / feminine</td><td>l'enfant</td></tr>
<tr><td>feminine</td><td>la fille</td></tr>
</table>

▲ The definite article changes in front of *à* or *de*.

	à	***de***
masculine singular	*à le → au*	*de le → du*
plural	*à les → aux*	*de les → des*

The indefinite article

The indefinite article is generally used with nouns referring to people or things that are not known exactly, that have not already been mentioned...

	singular	**plural**
masculine	*un homme*	*des amis*
feminine	*une femme*	

The partitive article

The partitive article expresses an undetermined quantity or number of the noun in question:
Je bois de l'eau ; je mange de la viande, du pain, des œufs...

▲ *Du, de la, des, de l'* change to *pas d'* in the negative:
Il y a du pain, de la viande, des œufs. → Il n'y a pas de pain, de viande, d'eau, d'œufs.

Omission of the definite article

Nouns are used without the definite article in the following cases :
– before "midi" (= midday) and "minuit" (= midnight);
– before the names of religious festivals (Noël - Christmas, Pâques - Easter...);
– after "il y a" and "il n'y a pas" (= there is/are; there isn't/aren't);
– with the names of people (Pierre Dupont), but the definite article is used when referring to a family : les Dupont = the Dupont family;
– with the names of cities: Paris, Marseille, unless the article is part of the name itself: La Rochelle;
– with the names of certain islands: Cuba, Chypre, Maurice (but la Corse, la Sardaigne, les Açores...).

Demonstrative adjectives

	singular	plural
masculine	*ce livre* *cet homme*	*ces hommes*
feminine	*cette femme*	*ces femmes*

▲ *Cet* and *cette* have the same pronunciation.
Ce becomes *cet* in front of masculine nouns beginning with a silent *h*.
Demonstrative adjectives may be emphasized by adding *ci* or *là* (equivalent of the English "this" and "that"):

Donnez-moi ce livre-ci et cette revue-là.

Possessive adjectives

Possessive adjectives agree in gender and number with the noun.

	subject	1 object possessed		several objects possessed
		singular		plural
		masculine	feminine	
1 owner (singular)	1st 2nd 3rd	*mon* *ton* *son*	*ma* *ta* *sa*	*mes* *tes* *ses*
Several owners (plural)	1st 2nd 3rd	*notre* *votre* *leur*		*nos* *vos* *leurs*

Cardinal numbers

Cardinal numbers are invariable for gender with the exception of *un* → *une*.
Hyphens are used in compound numbers between 17 and 99 except where **et** is used: *vingt-deux, soixante-six,* but *quarante et un, cinquante et un...*

from 0 to 10	from 11 to 20	from 21 to 30
0 – zéro		
1 – un	*11 – onze*	*21 – vingt et un*
2 – deux	*12 – douze*	*22 – vingt-deux*
3 – trois	*13 – treize*	*23 – vingt-trois*
4 – quatre	*14 – quatorze*	*24 – vingt-quatre*
5 – cinq	*15 – quinze*	*25 – vingt-cinq*
6 – six	*16 – seize*	*26 – vingt-six*
7 – sept	*17 – dix-sept*	*27 – vingt-sept*
8 – huit	*18 – dix-huit*	*28 – vingt-huit*
9 – neuf	*19 – dix-neuf*	*29 – vingt-neuf*
10 – dix	*20 – vingt*	*30 – trente*

Multiples of ten

10 – dix	*60 – soixante*
20 – vingt	*70 – soixante-dix (60 + 10)*
30 – trente	*80 – quatre-vingts (4 x 20)*
40 – quarante	*90 – quatre-vingt-dix (4 x 20 + 10)*
50 – cinquante	*100 – cent*

How to form cardinal numbers:

– after 20, 30, 40, 50, 60, 80, form the numbers in the same way as in column "from 21 to 30".

□ ***Exceptions***

81 → *quatre-vingt-un*

101 → *cent un*

111 → *(the **et** disappears) cent onze*

– after 70 and 90, the numbers are formed as follows:

70 - soixante-dix	*90 - quatre-vingt-dix (4 x 20 + 10)*
71 - soixante et onze	*91 - quatre-vingt-onze (4 x 20 + 11)*
72 - soixante-douze	*92 - quatre-vingt-douze (4 x 20 + 12)*
73 - soixante-treize	*93 - quatre-vingt-treize (4 x 20 + 13)*
74 - soixante-quatorze	*94 - quatre-vingt-quatorze (4 x 20 + 14)*
75 - soixante-quinze	*95 - quatre-vingt-quinze (4 x 20 + 15)*
76 - soixante-seize	*96 - quatre-vingt-seize (4 x 20 + 16)*
77 - soixante-dix-sept	*97 - quatre-vingt-dix-sept (4 x 20 + 17)*
78 - soixante-dix-huit	*98 - quatre-vingt-dix-huit (4 x 20 + 18)*
79 - soixante-dix-neuf	*99 - quatre-vingt-dix-neuf (4 x 20 + 19)*

Fractions

1/2 → un demi *1/5 → un cinquième*
1/3 → un tiers *1/10 → un dixième*
1/4 → un quart
Un quart de beurre. Un demi-litre de lait.
Une carte routière au 1/200 000. (un deux cent millième)

Decimals

A comma is used in French where a decimal point would be used in English :

101,6 → cent un virgule six

Percentages

5 % → cinq pour cent
Les prix ont augmenté de 0,4 %. (zéro virgule quatre pour cent)

▲ *une dizaine* = a dozen (11 or 12...)
une centaine ≈ 100
but *une douzaine d'œufs = douze œufs.*

Adjectives of quality

• **Agreement in gender**

– Adjectives already ending in "e" in the masculine singular remain unchanged in the feminine and are pronounced the same: *aimable, facile...*

– When the masculine singular form of an adjective ends in a vowel other than "e" *(a, i, o, u)*, the feminine is formed by adding an "e" ; the pronunciation remains unchanged:
joli → *jolie ; nu* → *nue.*
– When the masculine singular form of an adjective ends in a consonant, the feminine is formed by adding the letter "e". If the final consonant is pronounced in the masculine, the pronunciation of the feminine form is identical :
direct → *directe.*
– If the final consonant of the masculine singular form is not pronounced, the addition of an "e" for the feminine form means that the final consonant must be pronounced :
petit → *petite ; gris* → *grise.*

▲ Some adjectives add an accent (è) in the feminine:
complet → *complète ; léger* → *légère*
Other adjectives double the final consonant before the "e":
bon → *bonne ; ancien* → *ancienne ; gros* → *grosse*

– Lastly, some adjectives change form (and pronunciation) in the feminine:
beau → *belle ; doux* → *douce ; fou* → *folle*
nerveux → *nerveuse ; neuf* → *neuve ; nouveau* → *nouvelle*

• **Agreement in number**
– The plural of adjectives is usually formed by adding an "s" to the singular form:
un homme aimable → *des hommes aimables*
– Some adjectives take an "x" in the plural:
un beau fruit → *de beaux fruits*
– Some masculine adjectives change their endings completely:
un homme normal → *des hommes normaux*
but *une femme normale* → *des femmes normales*

▲ Adjectives ending in "s" or "x" in the masculine singular do not change in the plural: *doux, heureux, bas, gros...*

• **Position of adjectives**
Adjectives of quality usually follow the noun: *un homme heureux*
Certain common adjectives, however, are usually placed in front of the noun: *beau, bon, petit, vieux, nouveau, faux...*
joli, mauvais, grand, jeune, vrai...
premier, deuxième, dernier...

COMPARATIVE OF ADJECTIVES

The comparative of superiority

This comparative is formed using "plus ... que" (= more ... than), as shown below :

plus + adjective + que

Les maisons sont plus chères que les appartements.

▲ **The comparative of superiority is contained in a single form of the adjective for:** *bon(ne) → meilleur(e)*
mauvais(e) → pire
(*"plus mauvais"* is also used)

The comparative of inferiority

This comparative is formed with the adverb "moins" (= less):

moins + adjective + que

Pierre est moins sympathique que son frère.

The comparative of equality

This comparative is formed with the adverb "aussi" (= as):
Lise est aussi belle que sa sœur.

SUPERLATIVE OF ADJECTIVES

The superlative relative

	superiority	**inferiority**
masculine (singular)	*le plus*	*le moins*
feminine (singular)	*la plus*	*la moins*
masculine and feminine (plural)	*les plus*	*les moins*

La femme la plus belle de la ville.
L'homme le moins beau de la ville.

▲ When the comparative is irregular, the superlative is also irregular:

bon(ne) → meilleur(e) → le(la) meilleur(e)

The superlative absolute

– "peu" (= little) is used to express a small degree:
Un étudiant peu intelligent.
– "assez" (= quite) is used to express a medium degree:
Un livre assez intéressant.
– "très" (= very) is used to express a large degree:
Une plage très tranquille.
– "trop" (= too) expresses excess :
Je suis trop fatigué(e) pour sortir ce soir.
– and the superlative can use combinations of the words listed above :
assez peu, très peu, trop peu… pas assez…

PRONOUNS

Personal pronouns

• **Subject pronouns**

		singular	**plural**
1st person		*je*	*nous*
2nd person		*tu*	*vous*
3rd person	masculine	*il*	*ils*
	feminine	*elle*	*elles*

The distinction between masculine and feminine only occurs in the 3rd person singular and plural.

▲ In compound tenses conjugated with the auxiliary "être", the past participle takes the feminine form if the personal subject pronoun denotes a feminine subject:

Vous êtes bien arrivés(es) ?

The subject pronoun «ils» is used to denote a group containing masculine and feminine subjects:

M. et Mme Laurent sont de Lyon. Ils ont deux enfants.

- **Direct object pronouns**

		singular	plural
1st person		*me (m')*	*nous*
2nd person		*te (t')*	*vous*
3rd person	masculine	*le (l')*	*les*
	feminine	*la (l')*	*les*

– Il voit souvent sa sœur ?
– Oui, il la voit toutes les semaines.

▲ The distinction between masculine and feminine only occurs in the 3rd person singular.

- **Indirect object pronouns**

	singular	plural
1st person	*me (m')*	*nous*
2nd person	*te (t')*	*vous*
3rd person	*lui*	*leur*

▲ The indirect object pronouns are identical to the direct object pronouns with the exception of the 3rd person singular and plural. There is no distinction between masculine and feminine.

Je lui parle. (Je parle à Jacques / à Marie.)
Tu leur écris. (Tu écris à Jacques et Paul / à Paul et à Marie / à Marie et à Anne.)

▲ In ordinary spoken French, the "e" of "*je, me, te, le*" is frequently not pronounced.

"J'le regarde. – Tu t'trompes."

- **Disjunctive pronouns**

Disjunctive (or "emphatic") pronouns are mainly used for emphasis :

Moi, je suis anglais.

		singular	plural
1st person		*moi*	*nous*
2nd person		*toi*	*vous*
3rd person	masculine	*lui*	*eux*
	feminine	*elle*	*elles*

Demonstrative pronouns

	singular		neutral	plural	
	masculine	feminine		masculine	feminine
simple forms	*celui*	*celle*	*ce (c')*	*ceux*	*celles*
compound forms	*celui-ci* *celui-là*	*celle-ci* *celle-là*	*ceci* *cela (ça)*	*ceux-ci* *ceux-là*	*celles-ci* *celles-là*

▲ The form with "là" is more common in ordinary spoken French. "Ça" is used more frequently than "ceci" or "cela", which are more common in the written language.

Le cinéma, j'adore ça !

Possessive pronouns

Possessive pronouns are used to avoid repetitions.

– C'est ton chien ?

– Oui, c'est le mien. (Oui, c'est mon chien.)

		WHAT IS POSSESSED			
		singular		plural	
		masculine	feminine	masculine	feminine
singular	1st	*le mien*	*la mienne*	*les miens*	*les miennes*
	2nd	*le tien*	*la tienne*	*les tiens*	*les tiennes*
	3rd	*le sien*	*la sienne*	*les siens*	*les siennes*
plural	1st	*le nôtre*	*la nôtre*	*les nôtres*	
	2nd	*le vôtre*	*la vôtre*	*les vôtres*	
	3rd	*le leur*	*la leur*	*les leurs*	

Relative pronouns

Simple forms:
" qui, que, quoi, dont, où "

- "qui" (= who, which) subject of the verb:
  Le boulevard qui est devant toi est le boulevard Montparnasse.
- "que" (= who(m), which) object of the verb:
  La maison que tu verras est celle du directeur de l'école.
- "quoi" (= what) :
  Je ne sais pas de quoi tu parles.
- "dont" (= of which, whose, about which):
  Voici le restaurant dont je t'ai parlé. (dont = le restaurant)
- "où" (= where):
  C'est le cinéma où nous avions rendez-vous. (où = le cinéma)

Compound forms:

	+ a	+ de
lequel	*auquel*	*duquel*
laquelle	*à laquelle*	*de laquelle*
lesquels	*auxquels*	*desquels*
lesquelles	*auxquelles*	*desquelles*

"En" and "y"

"En" and "y" refer to places :

– position (where you are) :
Il aime les Antilles, il y habite depuis vingt ans.

– direction (where you are going):
– Vous allez à Bordeaux cet été ?
– Oui, nous y allons en juillet.

– origine (where you are from):
– Quand êtes-vous allés(es) au Canada ?
– Nous en revenons.

The pronoun "en" is also used to denote a quantity :

– indeterminate:
Des pommes, vous en voulez combien ?

– precise (in this case "en" is combined with another element):
– Vous désirez combien de billets ?
– Donnez-m'en un.

Prenez ce livre et lisez-en une page.

"En" may also be used with an adverb of quantity such as "beaucoup, assez, trop, peu ...":
Des romans de Balzac, j'en ai lu beaucoup.

"Y" is also used in emphatic forms:
Les vacances ? J'y pense tout le temps !

ADVERBS

Formation of adverbs ending in "-ment":

lent (masculine adjective) → *lente* (feminine adjective)
lentement (adverb)

rapide (masculine or feminine adjective)
rapidement (adverb)

Some forms are more complicated :
fréquent → *fréquemment* ; *puissant* → *puissamment*

Position of adverbs in the sentence

When an adverb modifies an adjective or another adverb, it comes before that word :

Elle est assez jolie. (adverb + adjective)
Je dors très bien. (adverb + adverb)

When an adverb modifies a verb, it comes :

– after the verb if the verb is conjugated in a simple tense :
Il joue mal au tennis.

– usually between the auxiliary and the past participle if the verb is conjugated in a compound tense:
Nous sommes déjà allé(e)s voir ce spectacle.

VERBS

Conjugations

Each form is made up of a stem and an ending:
*Nous aim**ons**.*
The verbs may be classified into three groups or conjugations:
– 1st conjugation: verbs ending in "-er". They are regular with the exception of "aller".
– 2nd conjugation: verbs ending in "-ir" (a few irregular verbs in this group).
– 3rd conjugation : other, so-called irregular verbs.

Tenses and moods

• **The present indicative describes**

– the action at the moment of speaking:
Je chante. (en ce moment)

– regular, repeated actions:
Il chante tous les matins.

– an action in the immediate future:
Demain, j'arrête de fumer !

– an order :
Tu viens avec moi !

• **The perfect tense** ("passé composé")

– It is used with single past actions that have been completed:
Hier nous avons fait les courses.

Construction :

subject + auxiliary ("être" or "avoir") + past participle

The vast majority of verbs are conjugated with "avoir" in the perfect tense. The past participle is invariable except when the direct object is placed before the verb. The past participle then agrees with it in gender and in number :
Voilà les photos qu'on m'a données pour toi.

The verbs "aller (= to go), venir (= to come), sortir (= to go out), monter (= to go up), descendre (= to go down), partir (= to leave), arriver (= to arrive), rester (= to remain), devenir (= to become), naître (= to be born), mourir (= to die)" and all reflexive verbs are conjugated with the auxiliary "être":
Ils se sont rencontrés. Elles se sont rencontrées.

The past participle of these verbs agrees in gender and number with the subject of the verb. With reflexive verbs, however, the past participle only agrees if the object pronoun is a direct object of the verb:
Elles se sont habillées.
but *Elles se sont acheté des chaussures. (se = à elles-mêmes)*

• **The imperfect**

– Circumstances of a past event:
Il pleuvait quand je suis parti(e).

– Description of a past state:
Il faisait beau.

– Habitual or repeated actions in the past:
J'allais en ville tous les jours.

The perfect tense describes short, specific actions that happened in the past whereas the imperfect is used with actions that continued over a period of time. When used together in the same sentence, the imperfect describes the "background situation" providing a framework for the specific action in the perfect tense :

Le chien aboyait quand je suis entré(e).

- **The imperative**

The imperative is used to give commands, invitations, instructions, to make suggestions or requests.
It only exists in three persons: tu, nous, vous.
The forms are identical to those of the present indicative (except for 1st conjugation verbs where the "tu" form drops the "s") :

Regarde.	*Ne regarde pas.*
Regardons.	*Ne regardons pas.*
Regardez.	*Ne regardez pas.*

- **The conditional**

The conditional is the mood expressing uncertainty.

– It expresses an action liable to happen:
Si j'étais riche, j'achèterais une maison.

– a hypothesis:
Un accident de la route aurait eu lieu la nuit dernière.

– indirect questions or reported speech:
Elle a dit qu'elle rentrerait tard.

- **The subjunctive**

The subjunctive is a mood - a form of the verb related to the meaning of the sentence.
It expresses doubt, possibility, subjectivity.
When it is used to express a wish, obligation or order, it is usually preceded by "que":
Il faut que j'aille à la boulangerie.

The subjunctive mood is used after :
– " il vaut (mieux) que" : *Le temps est nuageux, il vaut mieux que tu prennes ton parapluie.*

– "il faut que" :
Il faut que nous allions rendre visite à un ami à l'hôpital.

– a main verb, in the negative, expressing an opinion :
Je ne pense pas qu'elle vienne.
Je ne crois pas qu'ils comprennent.
Je n'imagine pas que tu réussisses.

Verb tables

INFINITIVE	INDICATIVE		
	Present	**Imperfect**	**Future**
être *to be*	je suis tu es il est nous sommes vous êtes ils sont	j'étais tu étais il était nous étions vous étiez ils étaient	je serai tu seras il sera nous serons vous serez ils seront
avoir *to have*	j'ai tu as il a nous avons vous avez ils ont	j'avais tu avais il avait nous avions vous aviez ils avaient	j'aurai tu auras il aura nous aurons vous aurez ils auront
aller *to go*	je vais tu vas il va nous allons vous allez ils vont	j'allais tu allais il allait nous allions vous alliez ils allaient	j'irai tu iras il ira nous irons vous irez ils iront
appeler *to call*	j'appelle tu appelles il appelle nous appelons vous appelez ils appellent	j'appelais tu appelais il appelait nous appelions vous appeliez ils appelaient	j'appellerai tu appelleras il appellera nous appellerons vous appellerez ils appelleront
attendre *to wait*	j'attends tu attends il attend nous attendons vous attendez ils attendent	j'attendais tu attendais il attendait nous attendions vous attendiez ils attendaient	j'attendrai tu attendras il attendra nous attendrons vous attendrez ils attendront

IMPERATIVE	CONDITIONAL	SUBJUNCTIVE	PARTICIPLE
Present	**Present**	**Present**	**Past/Pres.**
 sois soyons soyez	je serais tu serais il serait nous serions vous seriez ils seraient	que je sois que tu sois qu'il soit que nous soyons que vous soyez qu'ils soient	été étant
 aie ayons ayez	j'aurais tu aurais il aurait nous aurions vous auriez ils auraient	que j'aie que tu aies qu'il aie que nous ayons que vous ayez qu'ils aient	eu ayant
 va allons allez	j'irais tu irais il irait nous irions vous iriez ils iraient	que j'aille que tu ailles qu'il aille que nous allions que vous alliez qu'ils aillent	allé allant
 appelle appelons appelez	j'appellerais tu appellerais il appellerait nous appellerions vous appelleriez ils appelleraient	que j'appelle que tu appelles qu'il appelle que nous appelions que vous appeliez qu'ils appellent	appelé appelant
 attends attendons attendez	j'attendrais tu attendrais il attendrait nous attendrions vous attendriez ils attendraient	que j'attende que tu attendes qu'il attende que nous attendions que vous attendiez qu'ils attendent	attendu attendant

INFINITIVE	INDICATIVE		
	Present	**Imperfect**	**Future**
boire *to drink*	je bois tu bois il boit nous buvons vous buvez ils boivent	je buvais tu buvais il buvait nous buvions vous buviez ils buvaient	je boirai tu boiras il boira nous boirons vous boirez ils boiront
comprendre *to understand*	je comprends tu comprends il comprend nous comprenons vous comprenez ils comprennent	je comprenais tu comprenais il comprenait nous comprenions vous compreniez ils comprenaient	je comprendrai tu comprendras il comprendra nous comprendrons vous comprendrez ils comprendront
conduire *to drive*	je conduis tu conduis il conduit nous conduisons vous conduisez ils conduisent	je conduisais tu conduisais il conduisait nous conduisions vous conduisiez ils conduisaient	je conduirai tu conduiras il conduira nous conduirons vous conduirez ils conduiront
connaître *to know*	je connais tu connais il connaît nous connaissons vous connaissez ils connaissent	je connaissais tu connaissais il connaissait nous connaissions vous connaissiez ils connaissaient	je connaîtrai tu connaîtras il connaîtra nous connaîtrons vous connaîtrez ils connaîtront
croire *to believe*	je crois tu crois il croit nous croyons vous croyez ils croient	je croyais tu croyais il croyait nous croyions vous croyiez ils croyaient	je croirai tu croiras il croira nous croirons vous croirez ils croiront

IMPERATIVE	CONDITIONAL	SUBJUNCTIVE	PARTICIPLE
Present	**Present**	**Present**	**Past/Pres.**
bois buvons buvez	je boirais tu boirais il boirait nous boirions vous boiriez ils boiraient	que je boive que tu boives qu'il boive que nous buvions que vous buviez qu'ils boivent	bu buvant
comprends comprenons comprenez	je comprendrais tu comprendrais il comprendrait nous comprendrions vous comprendriez ils comprendraient	que je comprenne que tu comprennes qu'il comprenne que nous comprenions que vous compreniez qu'ils comprennent	compris comprenant
conduis conduisons conduisez	je conduirais tu conduirais il conduirait nous conduirions vous conduiriez ils conduiraient	que je conduise que tu conduises qu'il conduise que nous conduisions que vous conduisiez qu'ils conduisent	conduit conduisant
connais connaissons connaissez	je connaîtrais tu connaîtrais il connaîtrait nous connaîtrions vous connaîtriez ils connaîtraient	que je connaisse que tu connaisses qu'il connaisse que nous connaissions que vous connaissiez qu'ils connaissent	connu connaissant
crois croyons croyez	je croirais tu croirais il croirait nous croirions vous croiriez ils croiraient	que je croie que tu croies qu'il croie que nous croyions que vous croyiez qu'ils croient	cru croyant

INFINITIVE	INDICATIVE		
	Present	**Imperfect**	**Future**
dire *to say*	je dis tu dis il dit nous disons vous dites ils disent	je disais tu disais il disait nous disions vous disiez ils disaient	je dirai tu diras il dira nous dirons vous direz ils diront
écrire *to write*	j'écris tu écris il écrit nous écrivons vous écrivez ils écrivent	j'écrivais tu écrivais il écrivait nous écrivions vous écriviez ils écrivaient	j'écrirai tu écriras il écrira nous écrirons vous écrirez ils écriront
entendre *to hear*	j'entends tu entends il entend nous entendons vous entendez ils entendent	j'entendais tu entendais il entendait nous entendions vous entendiez ils entendaient	j'entendrai tu entendras il entendra nous entendrons vous entendrez ils entendront
essayer *to try*	j'essaie tu essaies il essaie nous essayons vous essayez ils essaient	j'essayais tu essayais il essayait nous essayions vous essayiez ils essayaient	j'essaierai tu essaieras il essaiera nous essaierons vous essaierez ils essaieront
faire *to do/make*	je fais tu fais il fait nous faisons vous faites ils font	je faisais tu faisais il faisait nous faisions vous faisiez ils faisaient	je ferai tu feras il fera nous ferons vous ferez ils feront
falloir *to be necessary*	il faut	il fallait	il faudra

IMPERATIVE	CONDITIONAL	SUBJUNCTIVE	PARTICIPLE
Present	**Present**	**Present**	**Past/Pres.**
dis disons dites	je dirais tu dirais il dirait nous dirions vous diriez ils diraient	que je dise que tu dises qu'il dise que nous disions que vous disiez qu'ils disent	dit disant
écris écrivons écrivez	j'écrirais tu écrirais il écrirait nous écririons vous écririez ils écriraient	que j'écrive que tu écrives qu'il écrive que nous écrivions que vous écriviez qu'ils écrivent	écrit écrivant
entends entendons entendez	j'entendrais tu entendrais il entendrait nous entendrions vous entendriez ils entendraient	que j'entende que tu entendes qu'il entende que nous entendions que vous entendiez qu'ils entendent	entendu entendant
essaie essayons essayez	j'essaierais tu essaierais il essaierait nous essaierions vous essaieriez ils essaieraient	que j'essaie que tu essaies qu'il essaie que nous essayions que vous essayiez qu'ils essaient	essayé essayant
fais faisons faites	je ferais tu ferais il ferait nous ferions vous feriez ils feraient	que je fasse que tu fasses qu'il fasse que nous fassions que vous fassiez qu'ils fassent	fait faisant
	il faudrait	qu'il faille	fallu

INFINITIVE	INDICATIVE		
	Present	**Imperfect**	**Future**
finir *to finish*	je finis tu finis il finit nous finissons vous finissez ils finissent	je finissais tu finissais il finissait nous finissions vous finissiez ils finissaient	je finirai tu finiras il finira nous finirons vous finirez ils finiront
lire *to read*	je lis tu lis il lit nous lisons vous lisez ils lisent	je lisais tu lisais il lisait nous lisions vous lisiez ils lisaient	je lirai tu liras il lira nous lirons vous lirez ils liront
manger *to eat*	je mange tu manges il mange nous mangeons vous mangez ils mangent	je mangeais tu mangeais il mangeait nous mangions vous mangiez ils mangeaient	je mangerai tu mangeras il mangera nous mangerons vous mangerez ils mangeront
mettre *to put*	je mets tu mets il met nous mettons vous mettez ils mettent	je mettais tu mettais il mettait nous mettions vous mettiez ils mettaient	je mettrai tu mettras il mettra nous mettrons vous mettrez ils mettront
neiger *to snow*	il neige	il neigeait	il neigera
ouvrir *to open*	j'ouvre tu ouvres il ouvre nous ouvrons vous ouvrez ils ouvrent	j'ouvrais tu ouvrais il ouvrait nous ouvrions vous ouvriez ils ouvraient	j'ouvrirai tu ouvriras il ouvrira nous ouvrirons vous ouvrirez ils ouvriront

IMPERATIVE	CONDITIONAL	SUBJUNCTIVE	PARTICIPLE
Present	**Present**	**Present**	**Past/Pres.**
finis finissons finissez	je finirais tu finirais il finirait nous finirions vous finiriez ils finiraient	que je finisse que tu finisses qu'il finisse que nous finissions que vous finissiez qu'ils finissent	fini finissant
lis lisons lisez	je lirais tu lirais il lirait nous lirions vous liriez ils liraient	que je lise que tu lises qu'il lise que nous lisions que vous lisiez qu'ils lisent	lu lisant
mange mangeons mangez	je mangerais tu mangerais il mangerait nous mangerions vous mangeriez ils mangeraient	que je mange que tu manges qu'il mange que nous mangions que vous mangiez qu'ils mangent	mangé mangeant
mets mettons mettez	je mettrais tu mettrais il mettrait nous mettrions vous mettriez ils mettraient	que je mette que tu mettes qu'il mette que nous mettions que vous mettiez qu'ils mettent	mis mettant
	il neigerait	qu'il neige	neigé
ouvre ouvrons ouvrez	j'ouvrirais tu ouvrirais il ouvrirait nous ouvririons vous ouvririez ils ouvriraient	que j'ouvre que tu ouvres qu'il ouvre que nous ouvrions que vous ouvriez qu'ils ouvrent	ouvert ouvrant

INFINITIVE	INDICATIVE		
	Present	**Imperfect**	**Future**
plaire *to please*	je plais tu plais il plaît nous plaisons vous plaisez ils plaisent	je plaisais tu plaisais il plaisait nous plaisions vous plaisiez ils plaisaient	je plairai tu plairas il plaira nous plairons vous plairez ils plairont
pleuvoir *to rain*	il pleut	il pleuvait	il pleuvra
pouvoir *to be able*	je peux tu peux il peut nous pouvons vous pouvez ils peuvent	je pouvais tu pouvais il pouvait nous pouvions vous pouviez ils pouvaient	je pourrai tu pourras il pourra nous pourrons vous pourrez ils pourront
préférer *to prefer*	je préfère tu préfères il préfère nous préférons vous préférez ils préfèrent	je préférais tu préférais il préférait nous préférions vous préfériez ils préféraient	je préférerai tu préféreras il préférera nous préférerons vous préférerez ils préféreront
recevoir *to receive*	je reçois tu reçois il reçoit nous recevons vous recevez ils reçoivent	je recevais tu recevais il recevait nous recevions vous receviez ils recevaient	je recevrai tu recevras il recevra nous recevrons vous recevrez ils recevront
répondre *to answer*	je réponds tu réponds il répond nous répondons vous répondez ils répondent	je répondais tu répondais il répondait nous répondions vous répondiez ils répondaient	je répondrai tu répondras il répondra nous répondrons vous répondrez ils répondront

IMPERATIVE	CONDITIONAL	SUBJUNCTIVE	PARTICIPLE
Present	**Present**	**Present**	**Past/Pres.**
	je plairais	que je plaise	plu
plais	tu plairais	que tu plaises	plaisant
	il plairait	qu'il plaise	
plaisons	nous plairions	que nous plaisions	
plaisez	vous plairiez	que vous plaisiez	
	ils plairaient	qu'ils plaisent	
	il pleuvrait	qu'il pleuve	plu
	je pourrais	que je puisse	pu
	tu pourrais	que tu puisses	pouvant
	il pourrait	qu'il puisse	
	nous pourrions	que nous puissions	
	vous pourriez	que vous puissiez	
	ils pourraient	qu'ils puissent	
	je préférerais	que je préfère	préféré
préfère	tu préférerais	que tu préfères	préférant
	il préférerait	qu'il préfère	
préférons	nous préférerions	que nous préférions	
préférez	vous préféreriez	que vous préfériez	
	ils préféreraient	qu'ils préfèrent	
	je recevrais	que je reçoive	reçu
reçois	tu recevrais	que tu reçoives	recevant
	il recevrait	qu'il reçoive	
recevons	nous recevrions	que nous recevions	
recevez	vous recevriez	que vous receviez	
	ils recevraient	qu'ils reçoivent	
	je répondrais	que je réponde	répondu
réponds	tu répondrais	que tu répondes	répondant
	il répondrait	qu'il réponde	
répondons	nous répondrions	que nous répondions	
répondez	vous répondriez	que vous répondiez	
	ils répondraient	qu'ils répondent	

INFINITIVE	INDICATIVE		
	Present	**Imperfect**	**Future**
rire *to laugh*	je ris tu ris il rit nous rions vous riez ils rient	je riais tu riais il riait nous riions vous riiez ils riaient	je rirai tu riras il rira nous rirons vous rirez ils riront
savoir *to know*	je sais tu sais il sait nous savons vous savez ils savent	je savais tu savais il savait nous savions vous saviez ils savaient	je saurai tu sauras il saura nous saurons vous saurez ils sauront
sortir *to go out*	je sors tu sors il sort nous sortons vous sortez ils sortent	je sortais tu sortais il sortait nous sortions vous sortiez ils sortaient	je sortirai tu sortiras il sortira nous sortirons vous sortirez ils sortiront
venir *to come*	je viens tu viens il vient nous venons vous venez ils viennent	je venais tu venais il venait nous venions vous veniez ils venaient	je viendrai tu viendras il viendra nous viendrons vous viendrez ils viendront
voir *to see*	je vois tu vois il voit nous voyons vous voyez ils voient	je voyais tu voyais il voyait nous voyions vous voyiez ils voyaient	je verrai tu verras il verra nous verrons vous verrez ils verront

IMPERATIVE	CONDITIONAL	SUBJUNCTIVE	PARTICIPLE
Present	**Present**	**Present**	**Past/Pres.**
	je rirais	que je rie	ri
ris	tu rirais	que tu ries	riant
	il rirait	qu'il rie	
rions	nous ririons	que nous riions	
riez	vous ririez	que vous riiez	
	ils riraient	qu'ils rient	
	je saurais	que je sache	su
sache	tu saurais	que tu saches	sachant
	il saurait	qu'il sache	
sachons	nous saurions	que nous sachions	
sachez	vous sauriez	que vous sachiez	
	ils sauraient	qu'ils sachent	
	je sortirais	que je sorte	sorti
sors	tu sortirais	que tu sortes	sortant
	il sortirait	qu'il sorte	
sortons	nous sortirions	que nous sortions	
sortez	vous sortiriez	que vous sortiez	
	ils sortiraient	qu'ils sortent	
	je viendrais	que je vienne	venu
viens	tu viendrais	que tu viennes	venant
	il viendrait	qu'il vienne	
venons	nous viendrions	que nous venions	
venez	vous viendriez	que vous veniez	
	ils viendraient	qu'ils viennent	
	je verrais	que je voie	vu
vois	tu verrais	que tu voies	voyant
	il verrait	qu'il voie	
voyons	nous verrions	que nous voyions	
voyez	vous verriez	que vous voyiez	
	ils verraient	qu'ils voient	

Mini-dictionary French-English English-French

abonnement	n.m.	subscription	33
abonner(s')	v.	to take out a subscription	33
aborder	v.	to approach	2
aboyer	v.	to bark	3
abstrait(e)	adj.	abstract	5
accueil	n.m.	welcome, reception	36
acheter	v.	to buy	22
acteur	n.m.	actor	37
action	n.f.	share (stock exchange)	7
addition	n.f.	bill	6
additionner	v.	to add up	27
administration	n.f.	administration	43
adorer	v.	to adore	2
aérogramme	n.m.	airmail letter	32
aéroport	n.m.	airport	41
affaire	n.f.	deal, bargain	4
affaires	n.f.	belongings	13
agence immobilière	n.f.	estate agency	23
agenda	n.m.	diary	12
agent de change	n.m.	stockbroker	7
âge	n.m.	age	13
agréable	adj.	pleasant	36
aimer	v.	to love	2
air	n.m.	air	26
ajouter	v.	to add	27
alcool	n.m.	alcohol	13
aller	v.	to go	28
alpinisme	n.m.	mountaineering	38
amant	n.m.	lover	2
ambulance	n.f.	ambulance	9
amende	n.f.	fine	29
amoureux(euse)	adj.	in love	2
animal	n.m.	animal	3
anniversaire	n.m.	birthday	16
annonce	n.f.	advertisement	33
annuaire	n.m.	(telephone) directory	39
antenne	n.f.	aerial	40
anticyclone	n.m.	anticyclone	25
août	n.m.	August	12
apéritif	n.m.	aperitif	21
appareil	n.m.	telephone	39
appeler	v.	to call	35
appeler(s')	v.	to be called	36

A-B

applaudir	v.	to applaud	37
apprécier	v.	to appreciate	17
apprivoiser	v.	to tame	3
après	adv.	after	28
aquarium	n.m.	aquarium	3
arbitre	n.m.	referee, umpire	38
arbre	n.m.	tree	26
architecture	n.f.	architecture	5
argent	n.m.	money	13
arrestation	n.f.	arrest	30
arrêt (d'autobus)	n.m.	(bus)stop	42
arrêter(s')	v.	to stop	42
arriver	v.	to arrive	36
arroser	v.	to water	26
article	n.m.	article	33
artisan	n.m.	craftsman	43
artiste	n.m.	artist	5
ascenseur	n.m.	lift	28
Assemblée nationale	n.f.	National Assembly	31
assurance	n.f.	insurance	45
attirer	v.	to attract	2
augmenter	v.	to increase	4
aujourd'hui	n.m.	today	12
auto(mobile)	n.f.	motorcar	45
automobiliste	n.m.	motorist	29
autorisé(e)	adj.	authorized	29
avaler	v.	to swallow	24
avant	adv.	before	28
averse	n.f.	shower, downpour	25
avril	n.m.	April	12
baccalauréat	n.m.	(equivalent GCE 'A' levels)	14
bagages	n.m.	baggage	13
baigner (se)	v.	to bathe	44
baisser	v.	to decline	4
baisse	n.f.	decline	7
balade	n.f.	stroll	44
balle	n.f.	ball (tennis, golf ...)	38
baptême	n.m.	baptism	34
barbe	n.f.	beard	10
baromètre	n.m.	barometer	25
bas	n.m.	stockings	18
bâtiment	n.m.	building	23
batterie	n.f.	battery	45

beau-père	n.m.	father-in-law	15
beaucoup	adv.	a lot	2
beaux-parents	n.m.	in-laws	15
bébé	n.m.	baby	15
belle-fille (la bru)	n.f.	daughter-in-law	15
belle-mère	n.f.	mother-in-law	15
bénéfice	n.m.	profit	7
bête	n.f.	animal, creature	3
bicyclette	n.f.	bicycle	38
bidon	n.m.	can	45
bienvenu(e)	adj.	welcome	21
bière	n.f.	beer	6
billet	n.m.	ticket	42
bistrot	n.m.	café, pub	6
boîte aux lettres	n.f.	letterbox	23
bosser	v.	to work (colloquial)	43
bouche	n.f.	mouth	11
boucher	n.m.	butcher	1
boulanger	n.m.	baker	1
boutique	n.f.	shop	1
bras	n.m.	arm	11
bronzer	v.	to get a tan	44
brosse	n.f.	brush	10
brouillard	n.m.	fog	25
brushing	n.m.	blow-dry	10
bureau	n.m.	office	32
cabine	n.f.	telephone box	39
câble	n.m.	cable (TV)	40
cadeau	n.m.	gift	21
cadre	n.m.	executive	7
café	n.m.	café, coffee	6
café-théâtre	n.m.	theatre workshop	37
cage	n.f.	cage	3
caisse	n.f.	cash desk, till	1
caissière	n.f.	cashier	1
calculer	v.	to calculate	27
calendrier	n.m.	calendar	12
caméra	n.f.	camera	40
campagne	n.f.	country, countryside	26
capot	n.m.	bonnet (car)	45
carafe	n.f.	carafe, decanter	6
caresser	v.	to stroke	3
carnet	n.m.	book of tickets	42

C

carte (bancaire)	n.f.	(banker's) card	4
carte de visite	n.f.	visiting card	36
carte	n.f.	map	8
carte orange	n.f.	season ticket	42
carte postale	n.f.	postcard	32
carton d'invitation	n.m.	invitation card	21
cassette	n.f.	cassette	40
cathédrale	n.f.	cathedral	34
catholicisme	n.m.	Catholicism	34
cave	n.f.	cellar	23
ceinture	n.f.	belt	18
ceinture de sécurité	n.f.	safety belt	45
célébrer	v.	to celebrate	16
célibataire	n.m.	single	13
centaine	n.f.	about one hundred	27
cérémonie	n.f.	ceremony	34
chaîne	n.f.	channel (TV)	40
chalet	n.m.	chalet	44
chaleur	n.f.	heat	25
chambre	n.f.	room	20
champignon	n.m.	mushroom	26
champ de courses	n.m.	racecourse	22
chance	n.f.	luck	22
changer (de bus, de métro)	v.	to change (buses, underground trains)	42
chanson	n.f.	song	5
chanteur	n.m.	singer	5
chapelle	n.f.	chapel	34
chariot	n.m.	trolley	1
chat	n.m.	cat	3
chauffeur	n.m.	driver	42
chaussée	n.f.	road, road surface	29
chaussures	n.f.	shoes	18
chef (de cuisine)	n.m.	chef	17
chef d'orchestre	n.m.	conductor	37
chemin	n.m.	path, way, road	8
chemise	n.f.	shirt	18
chercher	v.	to look for	8
cher	adj.	expensive	1
cheval	n.m.	horse	22
chien	n.m.	dog	3
chiffre	n.m.	figure, number	27
choisir	v.	to choose	6

chômeur	n.m.	unemployed person	43
christianisme	n.m.	Christianity	34
ciel	n.m.	sky	25
cigarettes	n.f.	cigarettes	13
cirque	n.m.	circus	37
ciseaux	n.m.	scissors	10
citoyen	n.m.	citizen	31
classe	n.f.	class	14
classique	adj.	classical	5
clé	n.f.	key	20
client	n.m.	customer	1
clignotant	n.m.	indicator	45
code	n.m.	code	28
cœur	n.m.	heart	24
coiffer	v.	to do sb's hair	10
colis	n.m.	parcel	32
collants	n.m.	tights	18
colonne	n.f.	column	33
combiné	n.m.	receiver	39
comédien	n.m.	actor	37
commander	v.	to order	20
commémorer	v.	to commemorate	16
commerçant	n.m.	shopkeeper	1
commissaire	n.m.	superintendent	30
commissariat	n.m.	police station (cities)	30
commune	n.f.	parish, borough	31
communication	n.f.	telephone call	39
compétition	n.f.	competition	38
composer	v.	to dial	39
compter	v.	to count	27
comptoir	n.m.	bar, counter	6
concert	n.m.	concert	37
concours	n.m.	competition	22
concubinage	n.m.	cohabitation	15
conducteur	n.m.	(engine) driver	42
conduire	v.	to drive	9
congé	n.m.	holiday	16
conjoncture	n.f.	situation, climate	7
connaître	v.	to know	21
connu(e)	adj.	known	36
consommateur	n.m.	consumer	1
consommation	n.f.	consumption	45
constat	n.m.	report	30

C-D

content(e)	adj.	pleased	36
contravention	n.f.	fine	30
contrôle (d'identité)	n.m.	(identity) check	30
contrôler	v.	to inspect	13
contrôleur	n.m.	(ticket) inspector	42
copain	n.m.	pal, friend	2
copropriété	n.f.	co-ownership	23
correspondance	n.f.	connection	42
costume	n.m.	suit	18
coter	v.	to quote, list	7
côté (à)	adv.	next to	8
coucher (se)	v.	to go to bed	19
courir	v.	to run	38
courrier	n.m.	mail	32
cours	n.m.	lesson, course	14
court(e)	adj.	short	10
cousin	n.m.	cousin	15
crâne	n.m.	skull	11
cravate	n.f.	tie	18
crédit (à)	n.m.	(on) credit	4
crédit	n.m.	credit	7
crémerie	n.f.	dairy	1
crème (café)	n.m.	white coffee	6
crevaison	n.f.	puncture	9
crime	n.m.	murder, crime	30
croire	v.	to believe	34
croque-monsieur	n.m.	toasted cheese sandwich with ham	6
croyant	n.m.	believer	34
cueillir	v.	to pick, gather	26
cuisinier	n.m.	cook	17
curé	n.m.	parish priest	34
curriculum vitae	n.m.	curriculum vitae	43
cycliste	n.m.	cyclist	29
danser	v.	to dance	21
danseur	n.m.	danser	37
danse	n.f.	dance	5
décembre	n.m.	December	12
déclarer	v.	to declare	13
décor	n.m.	scenery	37
décrocher	v.	to lift the receiver	39
déduire	v.	to deduct	27
défiler	v.	to march, parade	16
dégât	n.m.	damage	9

D

dégradé	n.m.	layered (hair)	10
degré	n.m.	degree	25
déguster	v.	to taste, savour	17
déjeuner	v.	to have lunch	19
délinquant	n.m.	delinquent	30
délit	n.m.	offense, crime	30
demain	n.m.	tomorrow	12
demander	v.	to ask for	6
démêler	v.	to untangle	10
demi (bière)	n.m.	half (of beer)	6
demi-heure	n.f.	half-hour	19
demi	n.m.	half	27
dents	n.f.	teeth	11
dépannage	n.m.	fixing (a breakdown)	9
département	n.m.	French administrative region	31
dépliant	n.m.	leaflet	41
dépression	n.f.	depression	25
député	n.m.	member of Parliament	31
dérangement	n.m.	out of order	39
derrière	adv.	behind	8
descendre	v.	to get off	42
déshabiller (se)	v.	to get undressed	18
dessert	n.m.	dessert	17
dessin	n.m.	drawing	5
détaillé(ée)	adj.	detailed	41
devant	adv.	in front of	8
déviation	n.f.	diversion	9
deviner	v.	to guess	22
dimanche	n.m.	Sunday	12
dîner	v.	to have dinner	19
dire (au revoir)	v.	to say goodbye	37
dire (bonjour)	v.	to say hello	37
directeur	n.m.	headmaster	14
direction	n.f.	direction	28
discipline	n.f.	discipline	14
distance	n.f.	distance	28
distribution	n.f.	distribution	33
diviser	v.	to divide	27
division	n.f.	division	27
divorcer	v.	to divorce	2
divorce	n.m.	divorce	15
divorcé(e)	adj.	divorced	13
dizaine	n.f.	about ten, dozen	27

doigt	n.m.	finger	11
domestiqué(e)	adj.	domesticated, tame	3
domicile	n.m.	address, home	23
donner	v.	to give	35
dos	n.m.	back	10
doubler	v.	to overtake	9
douche	n.f.	shower	20
douleur	n.f.	pain	24
douzaine	n.f.	dozen	27
draguer	v.	to chat up, pick up	2
dresser	v.	to train	3
droit (tout)	adv.	straight ahead	8
droite	n.f.	right	28
dune	n.f.	dune	44
échanger	v.	to exchange	4
échecs	n.m.	chess	22
écologie	n.f.	ecology	26
économie	n.f.	economy	7
écran	n.m.	screen	37
écrivain	n.m.	writer	5
éducation	n.f.	education	14
église	n.f.	church	34
électeur	n.m.	voter	31
élection	n.f.	election	31
élire	v.	to elect	31
élu	n.m.	elected representative	31
embrasser(s')	v.	to kiss	36
émission	n.f.	programme, broadcast	40
émotion	n.f.	emotion	2
emploi	n.m.	job, employment	43
employé	n.m.	clerk, employee	32
emporter	v.	to take away, prevail	7
enchanté(e)	adj.	enchanted	37
enfant	n.m.	child	15
enlever	v.	to take off	18
enquêter	v.	to inquire, investigate	35
enquête	n.f.	investigation	30
enregistrer	v.	to record	40
enseignant	n.m.	teacher	14
enseignement	n.m.	education, teaching	14
ensemble	n.m.	ensemble, outfit	18
entrée	n.f.	entry, entrance	5
enveloppe	n.f.	envelope	32

environnement	n.m.	environment	26
envoyer	v.	to send	32
épaule	n.f.	shoulder	9
épicerie	n.f.	grocery, groceries	1
épicier	n.m.	grocer	1
équipe	n.f.	team	38
erreur	n.f.	mistake	39
escalade	n.f.	(rock) climbing	44
escaliers	n.m.	stairs	23
espoir	n.m.	hope	22
essuie-glace	n.m.	windscreen wiper	45
est	n.m.	east	28
estomac	n.m.	stomach	9
étage	n.m.	floor, storey	28
études	n.f.	studies	13
examen	n.m.	exam	14
excuser(s')	v.	to apologize	35
expliquer	v.	to explain	35
exposition	n.f.	exhibition	5
express	n.m.	espresso (coffee)	6
face (en)	n.f.	opposite	8
facteur	n.m.	postman	32
faire l'amour	v.	to make love	2
faire l'honneur de	v.	to do (sb) the honour of	21
faire le plein	v.	to fill up (with petrol)	45
faire signe	v.	to make a sign	42
faner (se)	v.	to wilt	26
fanfare	n.f.	fanfare	16
fauteuil	n.m.	seat	37
femme de ménage	n.f.	cleaning lady	20
femme	n.f.	wife	15
fermeture	n.f.	closure	5
ferme	n.f.	farm	3
feu (rouge/vert)	n.m.	(red/green) traffic light	29
feu d'artifice	n.m.	fireworks	16
février	n.m.	February	12
fiancer(se)	v.	to get engaged	2
fidèle	n.m.	believer, faithful	34
filer	v.	to dash (past)	8
filet	n.m.	net	38
fille	n.f.	daughter	15
film	n.m.	film	37

F-G

fils	n.m.	son	15
fleur	n.f.	flower	26
fleuve	n.m.	river(major)	26
flipper	n.m.	pinball machine	22
flirter	v.	to flirt	2
foie	n.m.	liver	24
football	n.m.	football	38
forêt	n.f.	forest	26
forfait	n.m.	set price	42
format	n.m.	format	33
formulaire	n.m.	form	35
fouiller	v.	to search, go through	13
fraction	n.f.	fraction	27
freiner	v.	to brake	9
frein	n.m.	brake	45
frisé(e)	adj.	curly	10
froid	n.m.	cold	25
fromage	n.m.	cheese	17
front	n.m.	forehead	11
gagner	v.	to win	7
gain	n.m.	gain, earnings	4
galerie	n.f.	gallery	5
gants	n.m.	gloves	18
garage	n.m.	garage	23
garçon	n.m.	waiter	6
garde à vue	n.f.	police custody	30
gardien	n.m.	caretaker	23
garer (se)	v.	to park	29
gare	n.f.	station	41
gasoil	n.m.	diesel	45
gastronome	n.m.	gastronome	17
gauche	n.m.	left	28
geler	v.	to freeze	25
gendarmerie	n.f.	police station (country and	30
gendarme	n.m.	policeman small towns)	30
gendre	n.m.	son-in-law	15
genou	n.m.	knee	11
givre	n.m.	frost	25
gourmand	n.m.	gourmand	17
gourmet	n.m.	gourmet, epicure	17
goûter	n.m.	tea (afternoon snack)	21
goût	n.m.	taste	17
gouvernement	n.m.	government	31

French	Type	English	Unit
grands-parents	n.m.	grandparents	15
grasse matinée	n.f.	a long lie in (bed)	16
grave	adj.	serious	9
grève	n.f.	strike	43
gros lot	n.m.	first prize, jackpot	22
guichet	n.m.	ticket office	37
guide	n.m.	guide	17
gymnastique	n.f.	gymnastics	38
habiller(s')	v.	to get dressed	18
habiter	v.	to live in, occupy	23
hasard	n.m.	chance	22
hausse	n.f.	rise	7
hebdo(madaire)	n.m.	weekly magazine	33
hier	adv.	yesterday	12
hommage	n.m.	tribute, respects	16
homme d'affaires	n.m.	businessman	7
hôpital	n.m.	hospital	24
horaire	n.m.	timetable	14
horodateur	n.m.	parking meter	29
hôtesse	n.f.	hostess	21
hôte	n.m.	host	21
huile	n.f.	oil	45
île	n.f.	island	41
immeuble	n.m.	a building	28
impair(e)	adj.	odd (number)	27
imperméable	n.m.	raincoat	18
indicatif	n.m.	dialling code	39
indication	n.f.	information, directions	35
indice	n.m.	index	7
indiquer	v.	to indicate, show	28
information	n.f.	information	35
informer(se)	v.	to inquire	35
infos	n.f.	news	40
infraction	n.f.	minor offense	30
ingénieur	n.m.	engineer	43
inscrire(s')	v.	to join, enrol	38
inspecteur	n.m.	inspector	30
instituteur	n.m.	(primary school) teacher	14
interdit(e)	adj.	forbidden	29
interphone	n.m.	entry phone	28
interroger	v.	to question	35
investissement	n.m.	investment	7
invitation	n.f.	invitation	21

I-M

invité(e)	adj.	guest	21
islam	n.m.	Islam	34
itinéraire	n.m.	itinerary	41
jambe	n.f.	leg	11
janvier	n.m.	January	12
jardiner	v.	to do the gardening	26
jaune	n.m.	yellow	26
jeter	v.	to throw	26
jeton	n.m.	chip, token	22
jeudi	n.m.	Thursday	12
job	n.m.	temporary job	43
jouer	v.	to play	22
jour férié	n.m.	bank holiday	16
journal	n.m.	newspaper	33
journaliste	n.m.	journalist	33
judaïsme	n.m.	Judaism	34
juillet	n.m.	July	12
juin	n.m.	June	12
kiosque (à journaux)	n.m.	(newspaper) kiosk	33
laisse	n.f.	leash	3
laver	v.	to wash	10
lever (se)	v.	to get up	19
ligne	n.f.	line	39
lingerie	n.f.	lingerie, underwear	18
liquide (en)	n.m.	(in) cash	4
locataire	n.m.	tenant	23
location	n.f.	renting	23
loger (se)	v.	to find accommodation	23
loin	adv.	far	8
long(gue)	adj.	long	10
longer	v.	to border, go along	42
loterie	n.f.	lottery	22
lundi	n.m.	Monday	12
lycée	n.m.	secondary school	14
magasin	n.m.	store	1
magazine	n.m.	magazine	33
magnétoscope	n.m.	video cassette recorder	40
maillot (de bain)	n.m.	swimming costume	18
main	n.f.	hand	11
mairie	n.f.	town hall	35
maison	n.f.	house	23
mai	n.m.	May	12
maîtresse	n.f.	mistress	2

maître d'hôtel	n.m.	head waiter	20
maîtresse de maison	n.f.	hostess, housewife	21
majorité	n.f.	majority	31
malade	n.m.	invalid	24
malchance	n.f.	bad luck	22
mandat	n.m.	postal order	32
manger	v.	to eat	6
manteau	n.m.	coat	18
manucure	n.f.	manicurist	10
marchander	v.	to bargain over	4
marcher	v.	to walk, hike	44
mardi	n.m.	Tuesday	12
marée	n.f.	tide	44
mariage	n.m.	marriage, wedding	15
marié(e)	adj.	married	13
marier(se)	v.	to get married	2
mari	n.m.	husband	15
marron	n.m.	brown	26
mars	n.m.	March	12
maternelle	n.f.	nursery school	14
matières	n.f.	subjects	14
matinée	n.f.	morning	19
mécanicien	n.m.	mechanic	9
mécanique	n.f.	mechanics, mechanism	9
médecin	n.m.	doctor	24
médias	n.m.	the media	40
mensuel	n.m.	monthly magazine	33
mer	n.f.	sea	26
mercredi	n.m.	Wednesday	12
mère (maman)	n.f.	mother (mum)	15
message	n.m.	message	39
messe	n.f.	mass	34
métier	n.m.	trade	43
metteur en scène	n.m.	producer, film director	37
miauler	v.	to mew	3
micro	n.m.	microphone	40
midi	n.m.	midday	19
minuit	n.m.	midnight	19
minute	n.f.	minute	19
miser	v.	to stake	22
mise en scène	n.f.	production	37
moderne	adj.	modern	5
moment	n.m.	moment	19

M-O

moniteur	n.m.	instructor	44
montagne	n.f.	mountain	26
monter	v.	to get on	42
montre	n.f.	watch	19
monument aux morts	n.m.	cenotaph	16
mosquée	n.f.	mosque	34
motard	n.m.	motorcyclist	29
moustache	n.f.	moustache	10
multiplication	n.f.	multiplication	27
multiplier	v.	to multiply	27
muscle	n.m.	muscle	11
musée	n.m.	museum	5
nager	v.	to swim	38
naissance	n.f.	birth	15
natation	n.f.	swimming	38
national(e)	adj.	national	16
nationalité	n.f.	nationality	13
neiger	v.	to snow	25
neige	n.f.	snow	25
neveu	n.m.	nephew	15
nez	n.m.	nose	11
niveau	n.m.	level	9
nom	n.m.	name	13
nord	n.m.	north	28
normal(e)	adj.	ordinary	32
note	n.f.	bill	20
novembre	n.m.	November	12
nuage	n.m.	cloud	25
nuit	n.f.	night	19
numéro	n.m.	number	28
obligation	n.f.	bond	7
occupé(e)	adj.	engaged (telephone)	39
octobre	n.m.	October	12
office de tourisme	n.m.	tourist information	41
offrir	v.	to offer	21
oncle	n.m.	uncle	15
ongle	n.m.	fingernail	11
opérer	v.	to operate	24
opposition	n.f.	opposition	31
option	n.f.	option	14
orage	n.m.	storm	25
orchestre	n.m.	orchestra	37

oreilles	n.f.	ears	11
os	n.m.	bone	11
ouest	n.m.	west	28
ouverture	n.f.	opening	5
oxygène	n.m.	oxygen	26
P. V.	n.m.	parking ticket	29
page	n.f.	page	33
paiement	n.m.	payment	4
pain	n.m.	bread	6
pair(e)	adj.	even (number)	27
pancarte	n.f.	(road)sign	8
panne	n.f.	breakdown	9
panneau	n.m.	signpost	8
paquet	n.m.	packet, parcel	32
pare-brise	n.m.	windscreen	45
pare-chocs	n.m.	bumpers	45
parents	n.m.	parents	15
parier	v.	to bet	22
pari	n.m.	wager	22
parking	n.m.	car park	23
parlement	n.m.	parliament	31
parler	v.	to speak	39
parti (politique)	n.m.	(political) parti	31
parution	n.f.	appearance, publication	33
passager	n.m.	passenger	45
passage piétons	n.m.	pedestrian crossing	29
passage souterrain	n.m.	subway	29
passeport	n.m.	passport	13
passer	v.	to go past	8
passionnément	adv.	passionately	2
passion	n.f.	passion	2
pasteur	n.m.	minister	34
patient	n.m.	patient	24
pâtisserie	n.f.	cake shop, pastry	1
patron	n.m.	proprietor	6
pause	n.f.	break	19
payer	v.	to pay	1
peau	n.f.	skin	11
pedigree	n.m.	pedigree	3
peigne	n.m.	comb	10
peinture	n.f.	painting	5
pelouse	n.f.	lawn	26
pension (complète)	n.f.	(full) board	20

P

perdre (se)	v.	to get lost	8
père (papa)	n.m.	father (dad)	15
périodique	n.m.	periodical	33
permis (de conduire)	n.m.	(driving) licence	45
perspective	n.f.	outlook	7
perte	n.f.	loss	4
petits-enfants	n.m.	grandchildren	15
peu	adv.	a little	27
phare	n.m.	headlight	45
pharmacie	n.f.	chemist's	24
photo(graphie)	n.f.	photo(graph)	33
photographe	n.m.	photographer	5
pièce	n.f.	play	37
pied	n.m.	foot	11
piéton	n.m.	pedestrian	29
piqûre	n.f.	injection	24
piste	n.f.	track, (ski) run	44
pittoresque	adj.	picturesque	41
place	n.f.	seat	37
plainte	n.f.	complaint	30
plaire	v.	to please	2
plan	n.m.	(street) map, plan	42
plante	n.f.	plant	26
plat	n.m.	dish	17
pleuvoir	v.	to rain	25
pluie	n.f.	rain	25
plume	n.f.	feather	3
plus-value	n.f.	capital gain	7
plusieurs	adj.	several	27
pneu	n.m.	tyre	9
poids	n.m.	weight	32
poignée de main	n.f.	handshake	36
poil	n.m.	hair, coat (animal)	3
point de repère	n.m.	landmark	8
poisson (rouge)	n.m.	(gold)fish	3
poitrine	n.f.	chest	11
police-secours	n.f.	emergency services	30
politesse	n.f.	politeness, courtesy	36
pollution	n.f.	pollution	26
pont	n.m.	bridge	8
porter	v.	to wear	18
porter plainte	v.	to lodge a complaint	30
portière	n.f.	door	45

poster	v.	to post	32
poste	n.m.	post, police station	30
poste restante	n.f.	poste restante	32
poumon	n.m.	lung	11
pourboire	n.m.	tip	6
pourcentage	n.m.	percentage	4
pratiquer	v.	to be a churchgoer	34
précision	n.f.	further detail	35
préfet	n.m.	prefect (administrator of a *département*)	31
prénom	n.m.	first name	13
présentateur	n.m.	introducer, presenter	40
présenter (se)	v.	to introduce oneself	36
président	n.m.	president	31
prêtre	n.m.	priest	34
prévision	n.f.	forecast	25
prier	v.	to pray	34
primaire	n.m.	primary school	14
principal	n.m.	principal, headmaster	14
prise de sang	n.f.	blood test	24
privé(e)	adj.	private	40
prix	n.m.	price	4
produits (alimentaires)	n.m.	foodstuffs, produce	17
professeur (prof')	n.m.	teacher	14
profession	n.f.	profession	13
programme	n.m.	programme	37
promener (se)	v.	to go for a walk/ride	29
protestantisme	n.m.	Protestantism	34
province	n.f.	province	41
publicité	n.f.	advertising	33
pyjama	n.m.	pyjamas	18
quai (de gare)	n.m.	(station) platform	41
quart	n.m.	quarter	27
question	n.f.	question	35
queue	n.f.	queue	32
quotidien	n.m.	a daily (newspaper)	40
rabais	n.m.	discount	4
rabbin	n.m.	rabbi	34
race	n.f.	breed	3
radar	n.m.	radar	9
raide	adj.	straight, stiff	10
ralentir	v.	to slow down	9
rapide	adj.	fast, express	32

R

rapport	n.m.	report	30
raquette	n.f.	racket	38
raser	v.	to shave	10
rasoir	n.m.	razor	10
rayon	n.m.	department	1
réception	n.f.	reception	20
recette	n.f.	recipe	17
recevoir	v.	to receive	21
réclamations	n.f.	complaints	39
recommandé	n.m.	recorded (delivery)	32
récréation	n.f.	break, playtime	14
reçu	n.m.	receipt	32
rédacteur	n.m.	sub-editor	33
rédaction	n.f.	eitorial staff/offices	33
réduction	n.f.	reduction	4
réduit(e)	adj.	reduced	32
refuge	n.m.	refuge, mountain hut	44
régime (politique)	n.m.	(political) régime	31
régional(e)	adj.	regional	17
régler	v.	to settle	4
religieux(euse)	adj.	religious	16
rembourser	v.	to repay	4
remède	n.m.	remedy, medecine	24
remplir	v.	to fill out	13
rémunération	n.f.	remuneration	43
rendez-vous	n.m.	appointment	24
renseignements	n.m.	inquiries	39
renseigner (se)	v.	to make inquiries	41
réparation	n.f.	repair	9
repas	n.m.	meal	20
répondeur	n.m.	answering machine	39
répondre	v.	to answer	39
reportage	n.m.	report	33
repos	n.m.	rest	16
république	n.f.	republic	31
réservation	n.f.	reservation	20
réserver	v.	to book	20
résidence	n.f.	residence, residential flats	23
ressembler	v.	to look like	36
ressentir	v.	to feel	2
résultats	n.m.	results	22
retraite	n.f.	retirement	43
rétroviseur	n.m.	rear-view mirror	45

réveiller (se)	v.	to wake up	19
réveil	n.m.	alarm clock	19
revue de presse	n.f.	press review	40
rez-de-chaussée (rdc)	n.m.	ground floor	23
rincer	v.	to rinse	10
rivière	n.f.	river(minor)	26
robe	n.f.	dress	18
romantique	adj.	romantic	2
ronronner	v.	to purr	3
roue (de secours)	n.f.	spare wheel	45
rouler	v.	to go, run (of a car)	9
route	n.f.	road	9
rubrique	n.f.	column, section	33
sable	n.m.	sand	44
sac à dos	n.m.	rucksack	44
sac	n.m.	bag	1
sacrement	n.m.	sacrement	34
salaire	n.m.	salary	43
salle	n.f.	classroom	14
salon de coiffure	n.m.	hairdressing salon	10
samedi	n.m.	Saturday	12
sang	n.m.	blood	24
sauvage	adj.	wild	3
savoir	v.	to know	35
savoureux(euse)	adj.	tasty	17
sculpture	n.f.	sculpture	5
sèche-cheveux	n.m.	hair-drier	10
sécher	v.	to dry	10
secondaire	n.m.	secondary school	14
seconde	n.f.	second	19
secrétaire	n.f.	secretary	43
section	n.f.	section	14
sénat	n.m.	senate	31
sénateur	n.m.	senator	31
sens unique	n.m.	one-way street	29
sentiment	n.m.	feeling, sentiment	2
sentir (se)	v.	to feel	24
septembre	n.m.	September	12
serrer (la main)	v.	to shake hands	36
serveur	n.m.	waiter, barman	6
service (compris)	n.m.	service charge (included)	20
servir	v.	to serve	6
sexe	n.m.	genitals, sex	11

S-T

sieste	n.f.	siesta, snooze	19
signaler	v.	to signal	8
signalisation	n.f.	roadsigns, signposting	8
ski	n.m.	skiing, ski	38
skier	v.	to ski	44
slip	n.m.	underpants, panties	18
soigner	v.	to treat, look after	24
soir	n.m.	evening	19
soirée	n.f.	evening	19
soldes	n.m.	sale goods	1
sondage	n.m.	(opinion) poll	35
sonnerie	n.f.	ringing, bell	39
sortie	n.f.	exit	5
sortir	v.	to go out	21
souffler	v.	to blow	25
souffrir	v.	to suffer	24
soulager	v.	to relieve	24
soupe	n.f.	soup	17
sous-vêtements	n.m.	underclothes	18
soustraction	n.f.	substraction	27
soustraire	v.	to subtract	27
soutien-gorge	n.m.	bra	18
spécialiste	n.m.	specialist	43
spécialité	n.f.	speciality	17
sportif	n.m.	athletic (person)	38
stable	adj.	stable	7
stade	n.m.	stadium	38
stationner	v.	to park	29
station	n.f.	station	40
stationnement payant	n.m.	paying car park	29
studio	n.m.	one-room flat	23
sud	n.m.	south	28
suffrage (universel)	n.m.	universal suffrage	31
supérieur	n.m.	higher education	14
supporter	v.	to bear, put up with	24
surveillance	n.f.	surveillance	30
synagogue	n.f.	synagogue	34
syndicat d'initiative	n.m.	tourist information office	35
syndicat	n.m.	union	43
table	n.f.	table	20
tailleur	n.m.	suit (for women)	18
tante	n.f.	aunt	15
tard	adv.	late	19

tarif	n.m.	price list, rates	20
taxi	n.m.	taxi	42
teindre	v.	to dye	10
télécarte	n.f.	'phone card	39
télécopie	n.f.	fax	32
télégramme	n.m.	telegram	32
téléphérique	n.m.	cable-car	44
téléphoner	v.	to 'phone	39
température	n.f.	temperature	25
tempête	n.f.	storm	25
temple	n.m.	temple	34
temps	n.m.	time, weather	19
tension	n.f.	tension	7
terme	n.m.	term, deadline	7
terrasse	n.f.	pavement area (in front of café)	6
terroir	n.m.	soil, rural origin	17
tête	n.f.	head	11
thermomètre	n.m.	thermometer	25
thé	n.m.	tea	6
ticket (de caisse)	n.m.	receipt	1
tiercé	n.m.	(system of forecast betting)	22
timide	adj.	shy	36
tirage (gros/faible)	n.m.	(large/small) circulation	33
toilettes	n.f.	toilet	6
tôt	adv.	early	19
tourisme	n.m.	tourism	13
touriste	n.m.	tourist	41
train	n.m.	train	41
travailler	v.	to work	16
travail	n.m.	work	16
traverser	v.	to cross (over)	29
tricher	v.	to cheat	22
tromper (se)	v.	to dial the wrong number	39
trottoir	n.m.	pavement	8
trouver(se)	v.	to find oneself, meet	28
tutoyer	v.	to address sb using "tu"	36
tuyau	n.m.	tip (information), pipe	35
université	n.f.	university	14
urgence	n.f.	emergency	24
usine	n.f.	factory	43
vacances	n.f.	holidays	16
vaccin	n.m.	vaccine	3

V-W

valeur	n.f.	value	7
valise	n.f.	suitcase	13
valoir	v.	to be worth	1
variétés	n.f.	variety show	5
vendeur	n.m.	salesman	1
vendre	v.	to sell	4
vendredi	n.m.	Friday	12
vente	n.f.	sale	4
vent	n.m.	wind	25
verglas	n.m.	black ice	25
vert	n.m.	green	26
veste	n.f.	jacket	18
vétérinaire	n.m.	veterinary surgeon	3
veuf	n.m.	widower	13
vidéo	n.f.	video	40
vie sociale	n.f.	social life	21
villa	n.f.	detached house	23
village	n.m.	village	28
vin (blanc, rouge,rosé)	n.m.	wine (white, red, rosé)	17
visage	n.m.	face	11
visa	n.m.	visa	13
visite	n.f.	visit	16
visiter	v.	to visit	41
vite	adv.	fast	9
vivre	v.	to live	28
vœux	n.m.	(best) wishes	16
voie	n.f.	way, lane, track	29
voile	n.f.	sailing, sail	38
voiture (de train)	n.f.	(railway) carriage	41
volant	n.m.	steering wheel	45
voleur	n.m.	thief	30
volley	n.m.	volleyball	38
vomir	v.	to vomit	24
voter	v.	to vote	31
vote	n.m.	vote	31
vouloir	v.	to want	6
vouvoyer	v.	to address sb using "vous"	36
week-end	n.m.	weekend	16

ENGLISH / FRENCH

N.B. *To help you identify as quickly as possible the French translation of English verbs, we have grouped them together towards the end of the minidictionary after "to".*

about one hundred	centaine	n.f.	27
about ten	dizaine	n.f.	27
abstract	abstrait(e)	adj.	5
actor	acteur	n.m.	37
actor	comédien	n.m.	37
addition	addition	n.f.	27
address, home	domicile	n.m.	23
administration	administration	n.f.	43
advertisement	annonce	n.f.	33
aerial	antenne	n.f.	40
aeroplane	avion	n.m.	41
after	après	adv.	8
age	âge	n.m.	13
airmail letter	aérogramme	n.m.	32
airport	aéroport	n.m.	41
alcohol	alcool	n.m.	13
animal	animal	n.m.	3
animal, creature	bête	n.f.	3
answering machine	répondeur	n.m.	39
anticyclone	anticyclone	n.m.	25
aperitif	apéritif	n.m.	21
appointment	rendez-vous	n.m.	24
April	avril	n.m.	12
aquarium	aquarium	n.m.	3
architecture	architecture	n.f.	5
arm	bras	n.m.	11
arrest	arrestation	n.f.	30
article	article	n.m.	33
artist	artiste	n.m.	5
athletic (person)	sportif	n.m.	38
August	août	n.m.	12
aunt	tante	n.f.	15
authorized	autorisé(e)	adj.	29
baby	bébé	n.m.	15
back	dos	n.m.	11
bad luck	malchance	n.f.	22
bag	sac	n.m.	1
baggage	bagages	n.m.	13
baker	boulanger	n.m.	1
balcony	balcon	n.m.	23

B

ball (football, rugby ...)	ballon	n.m.	38
ball (tennis, golf ...)	balle	n.f.	38
bank holiday	jour férié	n.m.	16
baptism	baptême	n.m.	34
bar, counter	comptoir	n.m.	6
barometer	baromètre	n.m.	25
battery	batterie	n.f.	45
beard	barbe	n.f.	10
beer	bière	n.f.	6
before	avant	adv.	28
behind	derrière	adv.	28
believer	croyant	n.m.	34
believer, faithful	fidèle	n.m.	34
belongings	affaires	n.f.	13
belt	ceinture	n.f.	18
bicycle	bicyclette	n.f.	38
bill, invoice	facture	n.f.	39
birth	naissance	n.f.	15
birthday	anniversaire	n.m.	16
black ice	verglas	n.m.	25
block of flats	immeuble	n.m.	23
blood	sang	n.m.	24
blood test	prise de sang	n.f.	24
blow-dry	brushing	n.m.	10
bond	obligation	n.f.	7
bone	os	n.m.	11
bonnet (car)	capot	n.m.	45
book of tickets	carnet	n.m.	42
bra	soutien-gorge	n.m.	18
brake	frein	n.m.	45
bread	pain	n.m.	6
break	pause	n.f.	19
playtime	récréation	n.f.	14
breakdown	panne	n.f.	9
breed	race	n.f.	3
bridge	pont	n.m.	8
brown	marron	n.m.	26
brush	brosse	n.f.	10
building	bâtiment	n.m.	23
bumpers	pare-chocs	n.m.	45
businessman	homme d'affaires	n.m.	7
butcher	boucher	n.m.	1

C

cabaret	cabaret	n.m.	37
cable (TV)	câble	n.m.	40
cable-car	téléphérique	n.m.	44
café, coffee	café	n.m.	6
cage	cage	n.f.	3
cake shop, pastry	pâtisserie	n.f.	1
calendar	calendrier	n.m.	16
camera	caméra	n.f.	40
can	bidon	n.m.	45
capital gain	plus-value	n.f.	7
carafe, decanter	carafe	n.f.	6
caretaker	gardien	n.m.	23
car park	parking	n.m.	23
cashier	caissière	n.f.	1
cash desk, till	caisse	n.f.	1
casino	casino	n.m.	22
cassette	cassette	n.f.	40
cat	chat	n.m.	3
cathedral	cathédrale	n.f.	34
Catholicism	catholicisme	n.m.	34
cellar	cave	n.f.	23
cenotaph	monument aux morts	n.m.	16
ceremony	cérémonie	n.f.	34
chalet	chalet	n.m.	44
chance	hasard	n.m.	22
channel (TV)	chaîne	n.f.	40
chapel	chapelle	n.f.	34
cheese	fromage	n.m.	17
chef	chef (de cuisine)	n.m.	17
chemist's	pharmacie	n.f.	24
chess	échecs	n.m.	22
chest	poitrine	n.f.	11
children	enfants	n.m.	15
chip, token	jeton	n.m.	22
Christianity	christianisme	n.m.	34
church	église	n.f.	34
cigarettes	cigarettes	n.f.	13
circus	cirque	n.m.	37
citizen	citoyen	n.m.	31
civil	civil(e)	adj.	16
classical	classique	adj.	5
class	classe	n.f.	14

C-D

classroom	salle	n.f.	14
cleaning lady	femme de ménage	n.f.	20
clerk	employé	n.m.	32
closure	fermeture	n.f.	5
cloud	nuage	n.m.	25
club	club	n.m.	38
co-ownership	copropriété	n.f.	23
coat	manteau	n.m.	18
code	code	n.m.	28
coffee	café	n.m.	21
cohabitation	concubinage	n.m.	15
cold	froid	n.m.	25
column	colonne	n.f.	33
column, section	rubrique	n.f.	33
comb	peigne	n.m.	10
competition	concours	n.m.	22
competition	compétition	n.f.	38
complaint	plainte	n.f.	30
complaints	réclamations	n.f.	39
concert	concert	n.m.	37
conductor	chef d'orchestre	n.m.	37
connection	correspondance	n.f.	42
consumer	consommateur	n.m.	1
consumption	consommation	n.f.	45
cook	cuisinier	n.m.	17
country, countryside	campagne	n.f.	26
cousin	cousin	n.m.	15
craftsman	artisan	n.m.	43
credit	crédit	n.m.	7
curly	frisé(e)	adj.	10
curriculum vitae	curriculum vitae	n.m.	43
customer	client	n.m.	1
customer	client	n.m.	4
cyclist	cycliste	n.m.	29
dairy	crémerie	n.f.	1
damage	dégât	n.m.	9
dance	danse	n.f.	5
danser	danseur	n.m.	37
daughter-in-law	belle-fille (la bru)	n.f.	15
daughter	fille	n.f.	15
deal, bargain	affaire	n.f.	4
December	décembre	n.m.	12

decline	baisse	n.f.	7
degree	degré	n.m.	25
delinquent	délinquant	n.m.	30
department	rayon	n.m.	1
depression	dépression	n.f.	25
dessert	dessert	n.m.	17
detached house	villa	n.f.	23
detailed	détaillé(e)	adj.	41
dialling code	indicatif	n.m.	39
diary	agenda	n.m.	12
diesel	gasoil	n.m.	45
dinner	dîner	n.m.	21
direction	direction	n.f.	8
discipline	discipline	n.f.	14
discount	rabais	n.m.	4
dish	plat	n.m.	17
distance	distance	n.f.	28
distribution	distribution	n.f.	33
diversion	déviation	n.f.	9
division	division	n.f.	27
divorced	divorcé(e)	adj.	13
divorce	divorce	n.m.	15
doctor	médecin	n.m.	24
dog	chien	n.m.	3
domesticated, tame	domestiqué(e)	adj.	3
door	portière	n.f.	45
dozen	douzaine	n.f.	27
drawing	dessin	n.m.	5
dress	robe	n.f.	18
driver	chauffeur	n.m.	42
dune	dune	n.f.	44
early	tôt	adv.	19
ears	oreilles	n.f.	11
east	est	n.m.	28
ecology	écologie	n.f.	26
economy	économie	n.f.	7
education	éducation	n.f.	14
elected representative	élu	n.m.	31
election	élection	n.f.	31
emergency	urgence	n.f.	24
emergency services	police-secours	n.f.	30
emotion	émotion	n.f.	2

employee	employé	n.m.	43
enchanted	enchanté(e)	adj.	36
engaged (telephone)	occupé(e)	adj.	39
engineer	ingénieur	n.m.	43
ensemble	ensemble	n.m.	18
entry,entrance	entrée	n.f.	5
entry phone	interphone	n.m.	28
envelope	enveloppe	n.f.	32
environment	environnement	n.m.	26
espresso (coffee)	express	n.m.	6
estate agency	agence immobilière	n.f.	23
even (number)	pair(e)	adj.	27
evening	soirée	n.f.	19
evening performance	soirée	n.f.	37
exam	examen	n.m.	14
executive	cadre	n.m.	7
exhibition	exposition	n.f.	5
exit	sortie	n.f.	5
expensive	cher	adj.	1
face	visage	n.m.	11
factory	usine	n.f.	43
fair, charity fête	kermesse	n.f.	16
fanfare	fanfare	n.f.	16
farm	ferme	n.f.	3
far	loin	adv.	8
fast	vite	adv.	9
fast, express	rapide	adj.	32
father (dad)	père (papa)	n.m.	15
father-in-law	beau-père	n.m.	15
fax	télécopie	n.f.	32
feather	plume	n.f.	3
February	février	n.m.	12
feeling, sentiment	sentiment	n.m.	2
figure, number	chiffre	n.m.	27
film	film	n.m.	37
fine	contravention	n.f.	30
finger	doigt	n.m.	11
fingernail	ongle	n.m.	11
fireworks	feu d'artifice	n.m.	16
first name	prénom	n.m.	36
first prize, jackpot	gros lot	n.m.	22
fixing (a breakdown)	dépannage	n.m.	9

floor, storey	étage	n.m.	23
flower	fleur	n.f.	26
fog	brouillard	n.m.	25
foodstuffs, produce	produits (alimentaires)	n.m.	17
foot	pied	n.m.	11
football	football	n.m.	38
forbidden	interdit(e)	adj.	29
forecast	prévision	n.f.	25
forehead	front	n.m.	11
form	formulaire	n.m.	35
fraction	fraction	n.f.	27
French administrative region	département	n.m.	41
Friday	vendredi	n.m.	12
frost	givre	n.m.	25
further detail	précision	n.f.	35
gain, earnings	gain	n.m.	4
gallery	galerie	n.f.	5
garage	garage	n.m.	23
gastronome	gastronome	n.m.	17
genitals, sex	sexe	n.m.	11
gift	cadeau	n.m.	21
gloves	gants	n.m.	18
gourmand	gourmand	n.m.	17
gourmet, epicure	gourmet	n.m.	17
government	gouvernement	n.m.	31
grandchildren	petits-enfants	n.m.	15
grandparents	grands-parents	n.m.	15
green	vert	n.m.	26
grocer	épicier	n.m.	1
grocery, groceries	épicerie	n.f.	1
ground floor	rez-de-chaussée (rdc)	n.m.	23
guest	invité(e)	adj.	21
guide, guidebook	guide	n.m.	8
gymnastics	gymnastique	n.f.	38
hair, coat (animal)	poil	n.m.	3
hair-drier	sèche-cheveux	n.m.	10
hairdresser	coiffeur	n.m.	10
hairdressing salon	salon de coiffure	n.m.	10
half (of beer)	demi	n.m.	6
half-hour	demi-heure	n.f.	19
half	demi	n.m.	27
hand	main	n.f.	11

H-J

handshake	poignée de main	n.f.	36
head	tête	n.f.	11
headlight	phare	n.m.	45
headmaster	directeur	n.m.	14
head waiter	maître d'hôtel	n.m.	20
heart	coeur	n.m.	24
heat	chaleur	n.f.	25
higher education	supérieur	n.m.	14
holidays	vacances	n.f.	16
hope	espoir	n.m.	22
horse	cheval	n.m.	22
hospital	hôpital	n.m.	24
hostess	hôtesse	n.f.	21
host	hôte	n.m.	21
hostess, housewife	maîtresse de maison	n.f.	21
house	maison	n.f.	23
husband	mari	n.m.	15
in-laws	beaux-parents	n.m.	15
index	indice	n.m.	7
indicator	clignotant	n.m.	45
injection	piqûre	n.f.	24
inquiries	renseignements	n.m.	39
inspector	inspecteur	n.m.	30
instructor	moniteur	n.m.	44
insurance	assurance	n.f.	45
introducer, presenter	présentateur	n.m.	40
invalid	malade	n.m.	24
investigation	enquête	n.f.	30
investment	investissement	n.m.	7
invitation	invitation	n.f.	21
in front of	devant	adv.	8
in love	amoureux(euse)	adj.	2
Islam	islam	n.m.	34
island	île	n.f.	41
itinerary	itinéraire	n.m.	42
jacket	veste	n.f.	18
January	janvier	n.m.	12
job, employment	emploi	n.m.	43
journalist	journaliste	n.m.	40
Judaism	judaïsme	n.m.	34
July	juillet	n.m.	12
June	juin	n.m.	12

key	clé	n.f.	20
knee	genou	n.m.	11
known	connu(e)	adj.	36
landmark	point de repère	n.m.	8
late	tard	adv.	19
lawn	pelouse	n.f.	26
layered (hair)	dégradé	n.m.	10
leaflet	dépliant	n.m.	41
leash	laisse	n.f.	3
left	gauche	n.m.	28
leg	jambe	n.f.	11
lesson, course	cours	n.m.	14
letterbox	boîte aux lettres	n.f.	32
level	niveau	n.m.	9
lift	ascenseur	n.m.	20
line	ligne	n.f.	39
lingerie, underwear	lingerie	n.f.	18
liver	foie	n.m.	24
long	long (longue)	adj.	10
long holiday weekend	"pont"	n.m.	16
loss	perte	n.f.	4
lottery	loterie	n.f.	22
lover	amant	n.m.	2
luck	chance	n.f.	22
lunch	déjeuner	v.	21
lung	poumon	n.m.	11
magazine	magazine	n.m.	33
mail	courrier	n.m.	32
majority	majorité	n.f.	31
manager	directeur	n.m.	43
manicurist	manucure	n.f.	10
March	mars	n.m.	12
marriage, wedding	mariage	n.m.	15
married	marié(e)	adj.	13
mass	messe	n.f.	34
May	mai	n.m.	12
meal	repas	n.m.	20
mechanic	mécanicien	n.m.	9
mechanics, mechanism	mécanique	n.f.	9
member of Parliament	député	n.m.	31
message	message	n.m.	39
microphone	micro	n.m.	40

M-O

midday	midi	n.m.	19
midnight	minuit	n.m.	19
minister	pasteur	n.m.	34
minor offense	infraction	n.f.	30
minute	minute	n.f.	19
mistake	erreur	n.f.	39
mistress	maîtresse	n.f.	2
modern	moderne	adj.	5
moment	moment	n.m.	19
Monday	lundi	n.m.	12
money	argent	n.m.	13
monthly magazine	mensuel	n.m.	33
mosque	mosquée	n.f.	34
mother (mum)	mère (maman)	n.f.	15
mother-in-law	belle-mère	n.f.	15
motorcar	auto(mobile)	n.f.	45
motorcycle	moto	n.f.	29
motorcyclist	motard	n.m.	29
motorist	automobiliste	n.m.	29
mountain	montagne	n.f.	26
mountaineering	alpinisme	n.m.	38
moustache	moustache	n.f.	10
mouth	bouche	n.f.	11
multiplication	multiplication	n.f.	27
murder, crime	crime	n.m.	30
muscle	muscle	n.m.	11
museum	musée	n.m.	5
mushroom	champignon	n.m	26
nationality	nationalité	n.f.	13
national	national(e)	adj.	16
nephew	neveu	n.m.	15
net	filet	n.m.	38
newspaper	journal	n.m.	33
news	infos	n.f.	40
next to	côté (à)	adv.	8
night	nuit	n.f.	20
north	nord	n.m.	28
nose	nez	n.m.	11
November	novembre	n.m.	12
number	numéro	n.m.	28
nursery school	maternelle	n.f.	14
October	octobre	n.m.	12

odd (number)	impair(e)	adj.	27
offense, crime	délit	n.m.	30
office	bureau	n.m.	43
oil	huile	n.f.	45
one-room flat	studio	n.m.	23
one-way street	sens unique	n.m.	29
opening	ouverture	n.f.	5
opera	opéra	n.m.	37
opposite	face (en)	n.f.	8
opposition	opposition	n.f.	31
option	option	n.f.	14
orchestra	orchestre	n.m.	37
ordinary	normal(e)	adj.	32
outlook	perspective	n.f.	7
out of order	dérangement	n.m.	39
oxygen	oxygène	n.m.	26
packet, parcel	paquet	n.m.	32
page	page	n.f.	33
painting	peinture	n.f.	5
pain	douleur	n.f.	24
pal, friend	copain	n.m.	2
parcel	colis	n.m.	32
parents	parents	n.m.	15
parish, borough	commune	n.f.	31
parish priest	curé	n.m.	34
parking meter	horodateur	n.m.	29
parking ticket	P. V.	n.m.	29
parliament	parlement	n.m.	31
party	soirée	n.f.	21
passenger	passager	n.m.	45
passionately	passionnément	adv.	2
passion	passion	n.f.	2
passport	passeport	n.m.	13
path, way, road	chemin	n.m.	8
patient	patient	n.m.	24
pavement	trottoir	n.m.	29
paying car park	stationnement payant	n.m.	29
payment	paiement	n.m.	4
pedestrian	piéton	n.m.	29
pedestrian crossing	passage piétons	n.m.	29
pedigree	pedigree	n.m.	3
percentage	pourcentage	n.m.	7

P-Q

periodical	périodique	n.m.	33
phone card	télécarte	n.f.	39
photo(graph)	photo(graphie)	n.f.	33
photographer	photographe	n.m.	5
picturesque	pittoresque	adj.	41
pinball machine	flipper	n.m.	22
plant	plante	n.f.	26
play	pièce	n.f.	37
pleasant	agréable	adj.	36
pleased	content(e)	adj.	36
policeman (country and small towns)	gendarme	n.m.	30
police custody	garde à vue	n.f.	30
police station (cities)	commissariat	n.m.	30
politeness, courtesy	politesse	n.f.	36
pollution	pollution	n.f.	26
post, police station	poste	n.m.	30
postal order	mandat	n.m.	32
postcard	carte postale	n.f.	32
poste restante	poste restante	n.f.	32
postman	facteur	n.m.	32
prefect (administrator of a département)	préfet	n.m.	31
president	président	n.m.	31
press review	revue de presse	n.f.	40
price	prix	n.m.	4
price list, rate	tarif	n.m.	32
priest	prêtre	n.m.	34
primary school	primaire	n.m.	14
principal, headmaster	principal	n.m.	14
private	privé(e)	adj.	40
producer, film director	metteur en scène	n.m.	37
production	mise en scène	n,f.	37
profession	profession	n.f.	36
profit	bénéfice	n.m.	7
programme, broadcast	émission	n.f.	40
proprietor	patron	n.m.	6
Protestantism	protestantisme	n.m.	34
province	province	n.f.	41
puncture	crevaison	n.f.	9
pyjamas	pyjama	n.m.	18
quarter	quart	n.m.	27

rabbi	rabbin	n.m.	34
racecourse	champ de courses	n.m.	22
racket	raquette	n.f.	38
raincoat	imperméable	n.m.	18
rain	pluie	n.f.	25
razor	rasoir	n.m.	10
rear-view mirror	rétroviseur	n.m.	45
receipt	ticket (de caisse)	n.m.	1
receiver	combiné	n.m.	39
recipe	recette	n.f.	17
recorded (delivery)	recommandé	n.m.	32
reduced	réduit(e)	adj.	32
referee, umpire	arbitre	n.m.	38
refuge, mountain hut	refuge	n.m.	44
regional	régional(e)	adj.	17
region	région	n.f.	31
religious	religieux(euse)	adj.	16
remedy, medecine	remède	n.m.	24
remuneration	rémunération	n.f.	43
renting	location	n.f.	23
repair	réparation	n.f.	9
republic	république	n.f.	31
reservation	réservation	n.f.	20
residence, residential flats	résidence	n.f.	23
resort	station	n.f.	44
rest	repos	n.m.	16
results	résultats	n.m.	22
retirement	retraite	n.f.	43
right	droite	n.m.	28
ringing, bell	sonnerie	n.f.	39
rise	hausse	n.f.	7
river(major)	fleuve	n.m.	26
river(minor)	rivière	n.f.	26
road	route	n.f.	9
road surface	chaussée	n.f.	29
roadsigns, signposting	signalisation	n.f.	9
romantic	romantique	adj.	2
room	chambre	n.f.	20
rucksack	sac à dos	n.m.	44
sacrement	sacrement	n.m.	1
safety belt	ceinture de sécurité	n.f.	45
sailing	voile	n.f.	44

S

salary	salaire	n.m.	43
salesman	vendeur	n.m.	1
sale	vente	n.f.	4
sale goods	soldes	n.m.	1
sand	sable	n.m.	44
Saturday	samedi	n.m.	12
scenery	décor	n.m.	37
scissors	ciseaux	n.m.	10
screen	écran	n.m.	37
sculpture	sculpture	n.f.	5
sea	mer	n.f.	26
season ticket	carte orange	n.f.	42
seat	place	n.f.	37
second	seconde	n.f.	19
secondary school	secondaire	n.m.	14
secretary	secrétaire	n.f.	43
section	section	n.f.	14
senate	sénat	n.m.	31
senator	sénateur	n.m.	31
September	septembre	n.m.	12
serious	grave	adj.	9
service charge (included)	service (compris)	n.m.	20
set price	forfait	n.m.	42
several	plusieurs	adj.	27
sex	sexe	n.m.	13
share (stock exchange)	action	n.f.	7
shirt	chemise	n.f.	18
shoes	chaussures	n.f.	18
shop	boutique	n.f.	1
shopkeeper	commerçant	n.m.	43
short	court(e)	adj.	10
shoulder	épaule	n.f.	11
shower	douche	n.f.	20
shy	timide	adj.	36
siesta, snooze	sieste	n.f.	19
signpost	panneau	n.m.	8
singer	chanteur	n.m.	37
single	célibataire	n.m.	13
situation, climate	conjoncture	n.f.	7
skiing, ski	ski	n.m.	38
skin	peau	n.f.	11
skull	crâne	n.m.	11

sky	ciel	n.m.	25
snow	neige	n.f.	44
social life	vie sociale	n.f.	21
soil, rural origin	terroir	n.m.	17
song	chanson	n.f.	5
son	fils	n.m.	15
son-in-law	gendre	n.m.	15
soup	soupe	n.f.	17
south	sud	n.m.	28
spare wheel	roue (de secours)	n.f.	45
specialist	spécialiste	n.m.	43
speciality	spécialité	n.f.	17
stable	stable	adj.	7
stadium	stade	n.m.	38
stairs	escaliers	n.m.	23
station	gare	n.f.	3
steering wheel	volant	n.m.	45
stockbroker	agent de change	n.m.	7
stockings	bas	n.m.	18
stomach	estomac	n.m.	11
store	magasin	n.m.	1
storm	tempête	n.f.	25
straight, stiff	raide	adj.	10
straight ahead	droit (tout)	adv.	8
strike	grève	n.f.	43
stroll	balade	n.f.	44
studies	études	n.f.	13
sub-editor	rédacteur	n.m.	33
subjects	matières	n.f.	14
subscription	abonnement	n.m.	33
substraction	soustraction	n.f.	27
subway	passage souterrain	n.m.	29
suitcase	valise	n.f.	13
suit	costume	n.m.	18
Sunday	dimanche	n.m.	12
superintendent	commissaire	n.m.	30
surveillance	surveillance	n.f.	30
swimming	natation	n.f.	38
swimming costume	maillot de bain	n.m.	44
table	table	n.f.	20
taste	goût	n.m.	17
tasty	savoureux(euse)	adj.	17

T

tea (afternoon snack)	goûter	n.m.	21
tea	thé	n.m.	6
teacher	enseignant	n.m.	14
teaching	enseignement	n.m.	14
team	équipe	n.f.	38
teeth	dents	n.f.	11
telegram	télégramme	n.m.	32
telephone	appareil	n.m.	39
telephone box	cabine	n.f.	39
telephone call	communication	n.f.	39
temperature	température	n.f.	25
temple	temple	n.m.	34
temporary job	job	n.m.	43
tenant	locataire	n.m.	23
tension	tension	n.f.	7
term, deadline	terme	n.m.	7
terrace	terrasse	n.f.	23
theatre workshop	café-théâtre	n.m.	37
thermometer	thermomètre	n.m.	25
the media	médias	n.m.	40
thief	voleur	n.m.	30
Thursday	jeudi	n.m.	12
ticket	billet	n.m.	42
ticket office	guichet	n.m.	42
tide	marée	n.f.	44
tie	cravate	n.f.	18
tights	collants	n.m.	18
time, weather	temps	n.m.	19
timetable	horaire	n.m.	42
tip (information), pipe	tuyau	n.m.	34
tip	pourboire	n.m.	6
to 'phone	téléphoner	v.	39
today	aujourd'hui	n.m.	12
toilet	toilettes	n.f.	6
tomorrow	demain	n.m.	12
tourism	tourisme	n.m.	13
tourist	touriste	n.m.	41
to add	ajouter	v.	27
to address sb using "tu"	tutoyer	v.	36
to address sb using "vous"	vouvoyer	v.	36
to add up	additionner	v.	27
to adore	adorer	v.	2

T

to answer	répondre	v.	39
to apologize	excuser(s')	v.	35
to applaud	applaudir	v.	37
to appreciate	apprécier	v.	17
to approach	aborder	v.	2
to arrive	arriver	v.	36
to ask (for)	demander	v.	35
to attract	attirer	v.	2
to bargain over	marchander	v.	4
to bark	aboyer	v.	3
to bathe	baigner (se)	v.	44
to believe	croire	v.	34
to bet	parier	v.	22
to be a churchgoer	pratiquer	v.	34
to be called	appeler(s')	v.	36
to bear, put up with	supporter	v.	24
to be worth	valoir	v.	1
to blow	souffler	v.	25
to book	réserver	v.	37
to border, go along	longer	v.	42
to brake	freiner	v.	9
to buy	acheter	v.	22
to calculate	calculer	v.	27
to call	appeler	v.	39
to celebrate	célébrer	v.	16
to change (buses, underground trains)	changer (de bus, de métro)	v.	42
to chat up, pick up	draguer	v.	2
to cheat	tricher	v.	22
to choose	choisir	v.	6
to commemorate	commémorer	v.	16
to count	compter	v.	27
to cross (over)	traverser	v.	29
to dance	danser	v.	21
to dash (past)	filer	v.	8
to declare	déclarer	v.	13
to decline	baisser	v.	4
to deduct	déduire	v.	27
to dial	composer	v.	39
to divide	diviser	v.	27
to divorce	divorcer	v.	2
to do (sb) the honour of	faire l'honneur de	v.	21

T

to do sb's hair	coiffer	v.	10
to do the gardening	jardiner	v.	26
to drive	conduire	v.	9
to drop	baisser	v.	4
to dry	sécher	v.	10
to dye	teindre	v.	10
to eat	manger	v.	6
to elect	élire	v.	31
to exchange	échanger	v.	4
to explain	expliquer	v.	35
to feel	sentir (se)	v.	24
to fill out	remplir	v.	13
to fill up (with petrol)	faire le plein	v.	45
to find	trouver	v.	35
to find accommodation	loger (se)	v.	23
to find oneself, meet	trouver(se)	v.	28
to flirt	flirter	v.	2
to freeze	geler	v.	25
to gain, earn	gagner	v.	7
to get a tan	bronzer	v.	44
to get dressed	habiller(s')	v.	21
to get engaged	fiancer(se)	v.	2
to get lost	perdre (se)	v.	8
to get married	marier(se)	v.	2
to get off	descendre	v.	42
to get on	monter	v.	42
to get undressed	déshabiller (se)	v.	18
to get up	lever (se)	v.	19
to give	donner	v.	35
to go	aller	v.	28
to go for a walk/ride	promener (se)	v.	29
to go out	sortir	v.	21
to go past	passer	v.	8
to go, run (of a car)	rouler	v.	9
to go to bed	coucher (se)	v.	19
to guess	deviner	v.	22
to have dinner	dîner	v.	19
to have lunch	déjeuner	v.	19
to increase	augmenter	v.	4
tourist information office	office de tourisme	n.m.	41
town hall	mairie	n.f.	35
to indicate, show	indiquer	v.	28

to inquire	informer(se)	v.	35
to investigate	enquêter	v.	35
to inspect	contrôler	v.	13
to introduce oneself	présenter (se)	v.	36
to join, enrol	inscrire(s')	v.	38
to kiss	embrasser	v.	2
to know	connaître	v.	21
to know	savoir	v.	35
to lift the receiver	décrocher	v.	39
to live	vivre	v.	28
to live in, occupy	habiter	v.	28
to lodge a complaint	porter plainte	v.	30
to look for	chercher	v.	8
to look like	ressembler	v.	36
to lose	perdre	v.	22
to love	aimer	v.	2
to make a sign	faire signe	v.	42
to make inquiries	renseigner(se)	v.	35
to make love	faire l'amour	v.	2
to march, parade	défiler	v.	16
to mew	miauler	v.	3
to multiply	multiplier	v.	27
to offer	offrir	v.	21
to operate	opérer	v.	24
to order	commander	v.	20
to overtake	doubler	v.	9
to park	stationner	v.	29
to pay	payer	v.	1
to pick, gather	cueillir	v.	26
to play	jouer	v.	22
to play, act, show (film)	jouer	v.	37
to please	plaire	v.	2
to post	poster	v.	32
to practise, play	pratiquer	v.	38
to pray	prier	v.	34
to purr	ronronner	v.	3
to question	interroger	v.	35
to quote, list	coter	v.	7
to rain	pleuvoir	v.	25
to receive	recevoir	v.	21
to record	enregistrer	v.	40
to relieve	soulager	v.	24

T

to repay	rembourser	v.	4
to reserve	réserver	v.	20
to rinse	rincer	v.	10
to run	courir	v.	38
to say goodbye	dire (au revoir)	v.	36
to say hello	dire (bonjour)	v.	36
to search, go through	fouiller	v.	13
to sell	vendre	v.	4
to send	envoyer	v.	32
to serve	servir	v.	6
to settle	régler	v.	4
to shake hands	serrer (la main)	v.	36
to shave	raser	v.	10
to signal	signaler	v.	8
to ski	skier	v.	44
to slow down	ralentir	v.	9
to snow	neiger	v.	25
to speak	parler	v.	39
to stake	miser	v.	22
to stop	arrêter(s')	v.	9
to stroke	caresser	v.	3
to subtract	soustraire	v.	27
to suffer	souffrir	v.	24
to swallow	avaler	v.	24
to swim	nager	v.	38
to take away, prevail	emporter	v.	7
to take off	enlever	v.	18
to take out a subscription	abonner(s')	v.	33
to tame	apprivoiser	v.	3
to taste	goûter	v.	17
to throw	jeter	v.	26
to train	dresser	v.	3
to treat, look after	soigner	v.	24
to untangle	démêler	v.	10
to visit	visiter	v.	41
to vomit	vomir	v.	24
to vote	voter	v.	31
to wake up	réveiller (se)	v.	19
to walk, hike	marcher	v.	44
to want	vouloir	v.	6
to wash	laver	v.	10
to water	arroser	v.	26

to wear	porter	v.	18
to wilt	faner (se)	v.	26
to win	gagner	v.	22
to work *(colloquial)*	bosser	v.	43
to work	travailler	v.	16
track, (ski) run	piste	n.f.	44
trade	métier	n.m.	43
train	train	n.m.	41
tree	arbre	n.m.	26
tribute, respects	hommage	n.m.	16
trolley	chariot	n.m.	1
Tuesday	mardi	n.m.	12
tyre	pneu	n.m.	9
tyre	pneu	n.m.	45
uncle	oncle	n.m.	15
underclothes	sous-vêtements	n.m.	18
underpants, panties	slip	n.m.	18
unemployed person	chômeur	n.m.	43
union	syndicat	n.m.	43
universal suffrage	suffrage (universel)	n.m.	31
university	université	n.f.	14
vaccine	vaccin	n.m.	3
value	valeur	n.f.	7
variety show	variétés	n.m.	5
veterinary surgeon	vétérinaire	n.m.	3
video	vidéo	n.f.	40
video cassette recorder	magnétoscope	n.m.	40
village	village	n.m.	28
visa	visa	n.m.	13
visit	visite	n.f.	16
visiting card	carte de visite	n.f.	36
volleyball	volley	n.m.	38
voter	électeur	n.m.	31
vote	vote	n.m.	31
wager	pari	n.m.	22
waiter	garçon	n.m.	6
waiter, barman	serveur	n.m.	6
waitress	serveuse	n.f.	17
watch	montre	n.f.	19
way, lane, track	voie	n.f.	29
Wednesday	mercredi	n.m.	12
weekend	week-end	n.m.	16

W-Z

weekly magazine	hebdo(madaire)	n.m.	33
weight	poids	n.m.	32
welcome	bienvenu(e)	adj.	21
welcome, reception	accueil	n.m.	21
west	ouest	n.m.	28
white coffee	crème (café)	n.m.	6
widower	veuf	n.m.	13
wife	femme	n.f.	15
wild	sauvage	adj.	3
wind	vent	n.m.	25
windscreen	pare-brise	n.m.	45
windscreen wiper	essuie-glace	n.m.	45
wine (white, red, rosé)	vin (blanc, rouge,rosé)	n.m.	17
work	travail	n.m.	16
writer	écrivain	n.m.	5
yellow	jaune	n.m.	26
yesterday	hier	n.m.	12
zoo	zoo	n.m.	3

GRAMMAR INDEX

		Lessons
A	Adjectives	
	– demonstrative	45
	– possessive	36
	– of quality	5-11
	Adverbs	37
	Articles	
	– definite	4-25
	– indefinite	4
	– partitive	24
	Avoir (verb)	10
C	Comparatives	23
	– irregular comparatives	18
	Conditional	6-43
	Conjunctions	15
E	*Être* (verb)	16
F	Future	6-39
	Future (immediate)	42
G	Gerund	29-33
I	Imperative	7-30-35
	Imperfect tense	3-22-26-35
	Infinitive	19-41
	Impersonal forms	12
	Interrogative form	10-20
N	Negation	13-14
	Nouns (gender of)	25
	Numbers	27

P

Passive voice 8
Past participle 34
Perfect tense 3-9
Personne 12
Plural of nouns 32
Pluperfect tense 26
Prepositions 28-38
Present indicative 2-10
Pronouns
– *en* 17
– *on* (indefinite) 21
– demonstrative 45
– disjunctive 21
– indefinite 4
– personal 20-29
– possessive 36
– relative 28-14
– *y* 17

Q

Quelqu'un 12

R

Recent past 38

S

Subject of the verb 31
Subjunctive 1-18
Superlative 5-22

T

"Tu" form 2

V

Vous 39
"Vous" form 2

INDEX OF SITUATIONS

(This index corresponds to the "How to say it!" sections in each lesson)

		Lessons
A	Addressing a customer (waiter)	6
	Addressing a waiter (customer)	6
	Advising	20
	Asking a head waiter for advice	17
	Asking about the weather	25
	Asking for a price	4
	Asking for a reduction	4
	Asking for advice	42
	Asking for information	35
	Asking if there are any seats left (theatre)	37
	Asking the price	32
	Asking the time	19
	Asking the way	28-29
	Asserting religious beliefs	34
	Asserting something forcefully	27
C	Choosing a means of transport	41
	Complaining	1-14
	Complaining about the weather	25
	Customs officer speaking to a traveller	13
D	Describing someone	10
	Disagreeing	31
	Drafting a classified ad	33-45
E	Encouraging	5
	Expressing a desire	43
	Expressing a negative opinion	40
	Expressing a preference	41
	Expressing a wish	43
	Expressing admiration	5
	Expressing an opinion about someone	11
	Expressing doubt	12
	Expressing one's fears	3
	Expressing one's feelings	2
	Expressing one's hopes	3
	Expressing one's ignorance	12-43
	Expressing one's opinion	7

	Expressing preferences	38-40
	Expressing surprise	22
	Expressing uncertainty	12
G	Giving advice	42
	Giving advice about clothes	18
	Giving instructions	1-10
	Giving orders	9
	Giving orders (police)	30
	Giving the time	19
	Greeting someone	15
I	Inviting someone	21
J	Judging someone	2
M	Making a choice	41
	Making a suggestion	20
	Making an offer	20
O	Offering (accomodation)	23
	Ordering a meal	17
P	Presenting one's best wishes	16
	Prohibiting something	8
R	Recommending	20
	Requesting a service	9
	Requesting assistance	9
	Reserving a seat (theatre)	37
S	Saying goodbye	36
	Saying what is possible	38
	Saying what you are going to do	44
	Saying what you believe	34
	Saying what you have done	44
	Saying what you want	32
	Saying you don't understand	29
	Suggesting a means of transport	8
T	Taking a stand (opinion)	31
	Talking about one's health	24
	Telling the way	28
U	Using the telephone	39
W	Welcoming someone	15
	Writing a personal letter	26
	Writing an official letter	14

INDEX OF THEMES

		Lessons
A	Accidents	9
	Accommodation	23
	Administration	31
	Advertising	38-45
	Animals	3
	Art	5
B	Bank holidays	16-34
	Bar	6
C	Car	9-29-45
	Cinema	37
	Clothes	18
	Correspondence	14-23-26
	Customs	13
D	Dates	12-16
	Days of the week	12
	Directions	27-28-29-41-42
	Divorce	15
	Doctor	24
	Drinks	6-17
E	Ecology	26
	Economy	7
	Education	14
	Elections	31
	Entertainment	37
F	Family	15-21-26
	Finance	7
	Food/meals	6-17-20-21
G	Games	22
	Games (of chance)	22
	Gastronomy	17-20
	Greetings	36
H	Hairdresser	10
	Holidays	19-38-44
	Hotel	20
	Human body	11-24
I	Information	35-41-42
	Invitations	21
L	Lottery	22
	Love	2

M	Marriage	2
	Metro	42
	Money	4-7
	Months	12
	Mountain	44
	Museum	5
N	Nature	27
	Newspapers	33-40
	Numbers	27
P	Paintings	5
	Parking	8
	Police	29-30
	Politics	31
	Post office	32
	Press	33
	Prices	4
R	Radio	40
	Recipes	17
	Religion	34
	Reservations	20
	Restaurant	6-17-20
S	School	14
	Sea	44
	Shopping	1
	Shops	1-4
	Sickness	24
	Sport	38
	Stock Exchange	7
T	Telephone	32-35-39
	Television	40
	Theatre	37
	Theft	30
	Timetables	19
	Tourism	13-17-19-35-41-44
	Town centre	8-29-42
	Town Hall	31
	Traffic	8-9-41
	Train	41
	Transport	8-41-42
W	Weather	25
	Wine	17
	Work	43